T OF THE STARS:
dest War

2
HIROYUKI MORIOKA

Seikai: Crest of the Stars 2
A Modest War
Written by Hiroyuki Morioka

Translation - Sue Shambaugh
English Adaptation - Benjamin Arntz
Lay Out Designer - Jennifer Carbajal
Graphic Designer - Christian Lownds
Fan Consultants - Troy Christopher Haskin
Daniel Bonnell (ACIDSTEALTH)
Larry S. Moreland II

Editor - Kara Stambach
Senior Editor - Nicole Monastirsky
Digital Imaging Manager - Chris Buford
Pre-Production Supervisor - Erika 'skooter' Terriquez
Art Director - Anne Marie Horne
Production Manager - Elisabeth Brizzi
Managing Editor - Vy Nguyen
VP of Production - Ron Klamert
Editor in Chief - Rob Tokar
Publisher - Mike Kiley
President and C.O.O. - John Parker
C.E.O. and Chief Creative Officer - Stuart Levy

Crest designs by Tomas Montalvo-Lagos,
based on the original designs by Toshihiro Ono

A  Novel

TOKYOPOP Inc.
5900 Wilshire Blvd. Suite 2000
Los Angeles, CA 90036

E-mail: info@TOKYOPOP.com
Come visit us online at www.TOKYOPOP.com

ISBN: 978-159816-576-0

First TOKYOPOP printing: January 2007
10 9 8 7 6 5 4 3 2 1
Printed in the USA

Table of Contents

Characters:

Jinto	Son of Planet Martine's president
Lafiel	Pilot trainee in the Abh Imperial Star Force and the empress' granddaughter
Klowal	Baron Febdash
Srguf	Klowal's father, formerly Baron Febdash
Seelnay	Vassal in Baron Febdash's family
Entoryua	Inspector in the Luna Vega City Police's Criminal Investigation Dept.
Kyte	Military Police Captain in United Mankind's peacekeeping force
Ramaj	Empress of the Abh Empire

Letter From the Editor:

Dear *Seikai: Crest of the Stars* Fan:

Thank you so much for continuing to support this space opera saga by purchasing A *Modest War*.

In the original Japanese version of these books, the Abh language (Baronh) was written in a smaller phonetic alphabet called *rubi* and placed above the regular narration's *kanji*. Such treatment was not possible in an English text format. Thanks to the dedicated work of our translator, rewriter, and fan consultants, our adaptation uses phonetic Baronh in parentheses next to the English counterparts in narration; Baronh is left untranslated when it occurs in dialogue so as to ensure the reader's suspension of disbelief. As you read, please check out the Notes and Glossary in the back of the book—the Abh have a complex culture, and Baronh proves quite a challenging language to master!

I'd like to take this opportunity to thank Tomas Montalvo-Lagos, who rendered such beautiful images for these books, inspired by Toshihiro Ono's art. In the first volume, he drew a military insignia with seven snakeheads to represent the badge worn by Spyunej Ramaj Elmita in the manga. In this volume, he drew Jinto's family crest, which depicts a furry flying fish found on Planet Martine. For the next crest . . . well, you'll have to check out the final book!

Feedback is always welcome at the TOKYOPOP message boards! Stay tuned for the third and final volume, *Seikai: Crest of the Stars 3: Return to a Strange World.*

Now please enjoy A *Modest War!*

Kara Allison Stambach
Junior Editor, Manga Novels

Previously, in Princess of the Empire:

During their conquest of the galaxy, the Abh sought unconditional surrender of Jinto Linn's home planet, Martine. His father, President Rock, relinquished control in exchange for the status of Abh nobility.

As Count of the Hyde Star System, Jinto boarded the *Gosroth*, a battleship bound for the Imperial capital in order to join the Star Force. En route, they encountered an enemy fleet.

Jinto and the empress' granddaughter, Lafiel, managed to escape in a shuttle and attempted to reach the nearby Safugnoff gate. However, when they stopped to refuel in Baron Febdash's territory, he took them prisoner.

The epic saga continues in *Seikai: Crest of the Stars'* second volume: *A Modest War.*

Who are the Abh?

Collectively, the Abh are a machine. They do not value their children, except as replacement parts.

What is the machine?

It is the Humankind Empire of Abh, which is a continual threat to wholesome human society. If we do not stop this machine, it will devour all other human societies.

Thus, the Abh must be destroyed.

—From a speech by Congressperson Fitzdavid at the United Mankind Central Council

The two visitors were giving Baron Febdash (Lyuf Febdak) a real headache.

In the short history of Baron Febdash's nation, a mere two hundred and twenty-six trips around its sun, there had been no trouble, no excitement, no reason to notice the baron's little territory (Lyumusko).

But now, there were notable visitors, and they were disturbing the peace.

One of them, Jinto Linn, was stuck in a room with the former baron.

"See that?" Former Baron Febdash (known as Lyuf Raika Febdak) indicated a thick, faux-marble door. "That's where they brought you in."

"Who did?"

"I'm not sure. As usual, I was engaged in a lengthy debate with my only friend, the liquor bottle. I thought I heard the door open, which hasn't happened in . . . oh, I don't know, probably thirty years. When I came out, there you were, lying on the automatic stretcher."

"Just me and the automatic stretcher?"

"Yeah, sort of. There were two Gosuk in the hallway outside—very pretty gals, both of them. Neither one of them said anything, but I could tell they wanted me to do something."

"So what did you do?" Jinto probed.

"Well, these creaky old bones managed to roll you off the stretcher onto the floor, at which point it retracted into the hallway, and the door closed. The whole time, the Gosuk never said a word. Didn't even blink! For all we know, they could still be standing there!"

"And I was unconscious through out all this?" Jinto inquired, trying to prevent a lengthy digression from the old man.

"At first, Faneb, I thought you were dead! But then you started twitching, and I knew you were going to be okay. So I somehow managed to carry you all the way to that bed, which was no easy feat, because you're really much heavier than you look." He paused, then said, "I thought some rest would do you good, and you'd wake up refreshed and happy. But when you woke up, you started shouting and accusing me of so many heinous crimes."

"I didn't shout," Jinto corrected.

"Either way, you sure shocked this old man, who was only trying to help."

"Sorry," Jinto apologized.

"No worries, Faneb. Upon closer inspection, you're not such a bad guy."

That said, Lyuf Raika moved on past the door, continuing the tour of his confinement area. Unlike the interior of the patrol ship *Gosroth*, there wasn't a lot to see, so the tour was pretty short.

There were four different rooms surrounding a small garden: a washroom, a bathroom, a kitchen, and a storage room for automatic mechanisms (Onhokia). From the garden, a short hallway led to the former baron's personal rooms.

"I can't believe there isn't a single window," Jinto mumbled upon reaching the last stop of the tour—the ex-baron's living room.

"That'd make it too easy to break out of here!" Lyuf Raika commented. "Besides, there's not much to see; on the other side of this area, it's all Basev. I'm not too keen on watching raw meat grow in cultivation tanks, are you?"

"No, I guess not."

"Besides, in the void of space, windows aren't as practical as these," the baron said, flipping a switch. On one of the walls there appeared some synthetic scenery of a land world (Nahen). Snowcapped mountains loomed beneath an azure sky.

"It's amazing," Jinto admired.

"What kind of backwoods place are you from? This technology is standard—even more ancient than I am!"

"It's not the technology that impresses me; it's the scenery," Jinto clarified.

"Oh, sorry," the former baron said, obviously not sorry at all.

"Doesn't it look a little bit strange to you? The sky's blue looks unusual for that high altitude, or else the clouds are hanging way too low."

"You must be a Nahen native to notice something like that. The Abh are much more romantic about it."

"So this is Abh romantic art?" Jinto asked.

"A Deilbisecks. He prospered as an artist even in the early days of the Frybar. He's well known for his reproductions of land-world scenery."

"So he's from the age of Goh Ramgokotot?" Jinto asked.

"Yes."

"That explains it, then." During Goh Ramgokotot, the Abh were space nomads, flying from colony to colony to engage in interstellar trade. It made sense that they didn't have as good a handle on Nahen scenery as someone born on a land world.

"Deilbesicks called this one 'Gaf Laka,' or 'Tall Mountain,' which doesn't strike me as the most creative title," the former baron assessed, "so I like to call it 'Bar Lepenu.' "

" 'Pride of the Abh'?" Jinto tested his vocabulary.

"Exactly! Nothing represents the Abh spirit quite like this picture," the old man asserted. "It gives you the feeling of being on top of the world. No matter how insignificant you actually are, when you look down on this mountain, you feel as proud as anyone, even Her Majesty the Empress. If you have nothing else in the world, at least you have pride. That's the spirit of the Abh! That's what it's all about!"

The old man was practically jumping around the room, he was so excited. "And my good-for-nothing son doesn't get it! Instead of climbing over a tall mountain, he'd rather dig a ditch under it. I may be a lander genetically, but my spirit is more Abh than that clod's!"

Lyuf Raika's rant reminded Jinto of a bear he once saw at the zoo in Count Vorlash's territory (Dreuhynu Vorlak). The large and powerful beast was normally docile. However, when something flipped its irritation switch, the massive creature became the nightmare-inspiring epitome of primal anger.

As the old man got more and more worked up, Jinto wished they weren't trapped in the same cage, so to speak.

"Lonyu Lyuf Raika," Jinto hailed him cautiously, "maybe we should get back to thinking about our escape."

"Oh. Right. Good thinking, Faneb." The old man plopped onto the couch; the outburst had obviously worn him out. "Just remember this, young man. If you're Abh, always raise your children to be proud. But you can't just tell them to have pride. I tried that with my son and as you can see it didn't work. Pride is like a virus; you have to catch it, and keep your Golkia close enough to infect them, too."

"I'll keep that in mind," Jinto said. *"If* we ever get out of here."

"You're right. Let's scheme." The former baron scratched his chin. "Any ideas?"

"Maybe we could break down this wall." Jinto rapped on the wall with Deilbesicks' *Tall Mountain*. "We could use one of the Onhokia or something."

"Then what? Even if we could break through, they'd spot us trying to pass through the Basev."

"True." Jinto reconsidered. "Well, how do they feed you? Does the food come through that door there?"

Lyuf Raika shook his head. "There's a huge automated refrigerator in the kitchen. It disappears through the wall once every ten days and reappears full of food."

"Can we hide in it and ride it out?"

"In theory, but it just stocked itself yesterday. Even if we ate like pigs, it'd take a few days to eat all that food. You don't want to hang out that long, do you?"

It was Jinto's turn to shake his head. "Can we move it from this side?"

"No, definitely not."

"Well maybe we could destroy it and get into that passageway somehow . . ."

"Those are all very good ideas, Faneb, but there's a reinforced door behind the box. We'd kill ourselves trying to break through it."

Jinto snapped his fingers. "What about the garbage chute? If we slide down it . . ."

"Be my guest. One thing, though—there's a pulverizer halfway down. On the bright side, by the time you get down to the trash pile, we can just stick you in an envelope and mail you wherever you want to go."

"Man!" Jinto hung his head. "Help me out, here. You must have thought about a way to escape at some point."

"Of course; it's my favorite hobby. The only reason I can spot the flaws in your plans is because I've very seriously considered each of those options myself."

"I knew it." Jinto furrowed his brow. "Well, what would you do if there were an emergency?"

"You mean if I got sick or something? I'd call on the Luode, and they'd come get me. I don't know, though; it's never come up."

"Wait—you're telling me you've got a comms device in here?" Jinto's spirits rose to *Tall Mountain* levels.

"Yes, but it only connects to Banzorl Garyuk. You probably won't be able to call your girlfriend, Feia Lartneir." He snickered at Jinto's reaction. "I mostly use the thing to complain about the food."

"So, what if one of us pretends to be sick, or, I don't know, starts a fire or something?"

"You don't give up easily, do you, Faneb?"

"It won't work?"

"No. For whatever reason, I've never been sick a day in my life. If I got sick all of a sudden, coinciding with your arrival . . . My son's not nice, but he's not stupid either."

"Well, what about me? I could get sick."

"Do you think he'd care?"

The realization that this was undeniably true depressed Jinto.

"Don't sweat it. I'm sure he's counting the days until I kick the bucket, too."

"So, a fire wouldn't do us any good either."

"Afraid not," the former baron concurred gravely.

Sinking into an incredible gloom, Jinto determined he needed to take a breather to renew his enthusiasm for escaping. Excusing himself, he went into the corridor where he stopped to admire some flowers that surrounded a pleasant pond.

In the middle of the pond there was a small, round island big enough to accommodate about ten regular-sized people. A white, rainbow-shaped bridge connected the island to the garden. From the middle of the bridge, Jinto peered into the water, scanning for any signs of life. He didn't spot any.

Frustrated, he looked to the ceiling, which was shaped like a dome. Jinto estimated its apex was probably five-hundred Daj up. Near the peak, there was a faint, circular line. It looked like an entrance of some sort.

"Lonyu Lyuf Raika!" Jinto shouted.

"What is it?" the old man asked, rushing in.

"What's that?" Jinto pointed at the circle. "Doesn't it look like a small vessel dock?"

"Oh, that." The old man squinted. "It's not a Lo. It's just a Baud to the dock."

"But this isn't the Bidaut area."

"Originally, this area was intended for receiving noble visitors; there used to be a Dobroria right there," explained Lyuf Raika, pointing to the island.

Upon a more-informed inspection, Jinto noticed that the door was directly above the island.

"I think the idea was to make lander guests more comfortable, hence the greenery. My mother liked the idea, even though she never had the chance to greet any guests. My damn kid tore down the Dobroria to keep me in here."

"Is the Baud still useable?" Jinto asked, pointing to the round door.

"Sure. You can open it manually from the inside. You'd probably have to destroy the safety device, but that wouldn't be hard. Why, what do you have in mind?"

"Isn't it obvious?" Jinto started to get excited. "We're going to leave through there!"

"Into the vacuum of space?"

Jinto mulled it over. "If we walk along the Lyumex's roof," he reasoned, "eventually, we'd come across the Pelia. Then, when we're in the little ship, we could fly to the Garish."

Lyuf Raika pitied Jinto, who was really trying very hard. "Unfortunately, there aren't any pressurized suits here."

"Well . . ." Jinto was not ready to concede defeat. "I mean, people can live in a vacuum for a short time."

"Do you even know where the Pelia is?"

"Yeah. It's in the Bidaut."

"Right. The spaceport," the old man said matter-of-factly. "That's a long way from here. It's just impossible."

"It could be docked closer." Jinto clung to the last shred of hope. "We should at least scout it out once."

"We can't do that. The ascent-descent tube simultaneously served as the Yadobel. If we open the Baud now, the atmosphere in here will leak out."

"We could close the airlock right away."

"Elementary physics! With the pressure from the leaking atmosphere, that would be like trying to push a Resii up a mountain."

Resigning himself to the fate of sharing a small space with a fanatical old man for an indefinite period of time,

Jinto's head drooped. True, Lyuf Raika was an agreeable codger, but Jinto sure didn't want to spend the rest of his days with him.

Besides, there was also Lafiel. Jinto hoped she was okay. If the baron had any sense at all, he wouldn't harm the Lartneir of the Frybar. But then again, a sensible person wouldn't put a military officer (Bosnal) under house arrest, either.

"Yes, we'll have to dock the Pelia at the Baud," Jinto mumbled.

"Right. But how? Telekinesis? Remote mind control?"

"Just let me think for one minute!" Jinto exploded. Realizing how sharply he'd spoken, he turned red. "Sorry, I got excited."

"No offense taken," the old man said calmly. "I probably don't have a lot of time left, so there's no sense wasting it getting upset. If you want my opinion, it's probably best to forget about the Baud. So tell me, Faneb . . . what else you got?"

"Don't move," Lafiel commanded, brandishing a laser pistol (Klanyu). "This territory is now under Labule occupation."

Beside Lafiel, Seelnay hoisted her gun too.

They were in a large room with visual displays on the walls. One wall depicted scenery from planet Febdash, and the others were a blur of rapidly changing numbers and drawings. Three Gosuk gaped at the intruders from their positions at their control consoles (Kuro).

"What is the meaning of this?" demanded the woman who was presumably in charge.

"Hands in the air, Greida!" Seelnay shouted excitedly.

"What do you want?" Greida asked, completely bewildered.

"I am Bene Lodair Nei-Dubresc Borl Paryun Lafiel, of the Rue Labule."

"Yes, I already knew that," Greida said, still quite confused.

The other Gosuk maintained similar expressions of bewilderment. Was this some kind of joke? Did members of the Imperial family (Fasanzoerl) think this kind of thing was funny?

Lafiel felt irritated. These Gosuk were obviously not abreast of the situation, and she would have to be the one to tell them.

"I've occupied the Banzorl Garyuk of Lyumex Febdak in order to carry out a Labule mission. Now, everyone raise both hands and stand up slowly."

Accustomed to following orders, the Gosuk obeyed. Lafiel edged away from the door. She didn't want to have her back to the entrance in case the Lyuf came crashing through with armed guards.

Although it was her first time ever holding a weapon, Seelnay remained remarkably calm, sticking right by Lafiel's side.

"Feia Lartneir," Greida pled, "Why are you doing this? If you want anything, you only have to ask."

"Okay. May I speak to Lyuf Raika, please? Or better yet, please release him and Jarluk Dreu Haider?"

Greida's face instantly hardened. "I cannot do that by myself; it's forbidden."

"Then I'm afraid I'll have to use force, Gosuk Ran," Lafiel announced. "So, forget the Lyuf's orders. I'm in charge now."

"Freeze, Kufaspia!" Seelnay yelled, firing her laser pistol. The resulting beam errantly struck the image of Planet Febdak on the wall.

In the commotion, Kufaspia grabbed a weapon from below her control console and pointed it at Seelnay. Instantly, Lafiel squeezed off a shot, hitting Kufaspia right in the hand.

Kufaspia shrieked as her gun fell harmlessly to the ground.

Seelnay retrieved it and brought it back to Lafiel, who instantly determined it was a paralysis gun (Ribwasia).

"If you have any other weapons, hand them over now," Lafiel ordered, nodding at Seelnay.

Catching the hint, Seelnay inspected the other control consoles.

"What's going on, Seelnay?" one of the vassals asked. "Is this for real?"

"Well you see, Alusa—" Seelnay began cheerfully, as if they were probably good friends in other circumstances.

"Despite what you may have heard about the Abriels," Lafiel butted in, "I don't shoot people for fun."

Greida sighed. "But Feia Lartneir, it's impossible to open the door to the retirement section."

"Is that so?"

"Yes. Without Fal Sif's permission, it can't be opened from the Banzorl Garyuk. Our master has to be in this room and use his own Saij Daifat and Saij Kimena."

"Seriously?" Lafiel pressed.

"Yes," Greida confirmed.

"Then can I at least speak to the prisoners, please?"

"Yes, certainly," Greida affirmed as she got up from the control console. "I'll connect you right away. One moment."

"Don't try anything funny."

"Got it." Greida edged sideways until she was able to poke at the buttons (Borsh) of the comms device.

Just then, the door opened. Instinctively, Lafiel pointed her gun at the door.

"Aha! There you are, Feia!" Lyuf exclaimed as he ran into the room, trailed by several armed Gosuk.

He stopped in his tracks when he saw Lafiel's gun pointed right at him.

"You're just in time, Lyuf," Lafiel greeted him. "I've been informed that we need your Kreuno to free Jinto. Your cooperation is greatly appreciated."

"What are you slugs doing?!" Klowal yelled at his armed accomplices. "Can't you see she's got a gun? Protect me already!"

Forming a wall between the baron and Lafiel, the servants-turned-soldiers raised their weapons.

"Unbelievable!" Seelnay cried. "Do you realize you're pointing guns at Her Highness the Princess?"

The Gosuk flinched.

"Seelnay's a filthy traitor," the baron announced.

Lafiel stepped forward to protect Seelnay. "Imperial citizen Fegdakupe Seelnay is loyal to the Frybar, and therefore under my protection."

"Oh, Feia Lartneir," Seelnay gushed, "that's the nicest thing anyone's ever said about me!"

"Please," the baron said, disgusted. "Feia Lartneir, you're being rude."

"I am grateful for your hospitality, but I still must leave at once."

"You can't do that."

"It's not up to you; I'm leaving. So, you'd better get Jinto in here right away, because he's going with me."

"You mean Lonyu Jarluker Dreu Haider?" The baron inquired. "I'm afraid that's impossible."

"Why?"

"Because he's a guest of my father's."

"Fine. Let me speak to your father."

"That is also an impossibility."

"Why's that?"

"You, dear Feia Lartneir, should understand that I'd like to keep family matters private."

"I don't care about your family's problems! I want to speak to Jinto!" Lafiel pointed her gun directly at the baron's face. "Do you want to start a war, Lonyu Lyum?"

"This is ridiculous," the baron spat. "If you kill me, you'll never be able to free Jarluk Dreu Haider."

"You admit he's a prisoner?"

"Sure, if that's what you want. I've got Jarluk Dreu Haider locked up. I admit it. Happy? This is my Garish, and I make the rules here."

"I will rescue Jinto, even if I have to destroy you and your mansion."

The Lyuf could tell it was not a bluff; Lafiel was both ruthless and honest.

"Fine!" the Lyuf said shrilly. "But I'm Bar Sif too, and I don't bend for anyone, so it looks like we've got ourselves an Abh stand-off."

Nobody could think of what to do. Normally, the Gosuk knew exactly how to respond to threats against their master. But in this case, the offender did have the noble title (Traiga) of Feia. There were many exchanges of nervous glances. Through it all, Seelnay remained chipper.

"Your Highness the Princess," Seelnay hailed. "Fegdakupe Alusa is on our side. She wants to serve Lartei Kryb."

"Okay," Lafiel agreed without taking her eyes off the baron. "Accepted, under the same conditions I set forth for you."

"Traitors!" the baron shouted.

"All right, Lyuf," Lafiel said, tightening her grip on the trigger, "I'm going to count to three, and while I do that, you're going to open the door to the 'retirement center' or whatever it is you call it."

"Never!" the baron yelled as he ducked for cover.

Although Lafiel could have shot the baron dead in his tracks, she hesitated just long enough for him to escape through the same door he'd come through. His bodyguards followed.

"Hold it!" Seelnay started to give chase.

"Forget it, Seelnay," Lafiel commanded. Lafiel didn't actually want to shoot the baron; if she did, the Gosuk might not be as cooperative as they had been up to that point, and there would likely be a messy battle.

"Yes, Feia Lartneir. But what should we do now?" Seelnay asked eagerly.

"First things first. You two," Lafiel said, indicating Greida and Kufaspia. "Are you going to behave?"

"I . . ." Greida struggled to finish her thought. "It's my duty to protect this place, but as long as Fal Sif isn't here, I will follow Feia's orders."

"I won't!" Kufaspia proclaimed. "I'm with Lonyu Lyum until my dying day!"

"You've always been such a suck-up," said Alusa, expressing years of pent-up resentment.

"Go take a long walk off a short Bidaut!" Seelnay yelled at Kufaspia.

"Easy there, Gosuk Ran," cooed Lafiel, before turning to Kufaspia. "You should go get that hand looked at."

Kufaspia stood, bowed (albeit scornfully), and said, "You're being completely unreasonable, Feia. I beg you to reconsider."

"To me, your master's the unreasonable one. Now, go." Lafiel waved Kufaspia out with her gun.

"Honorable Vassal," Lafiel addressed Greida, "please connect me to the ex-baron's comms device. Also, do you know where the Lyuf went?"

"I'll look into it," Alusa said, returning to her Kuro.

Offering the comms device to Lafiel, Greida announced that she'd established a connection. It was a primitive device that didn't even have a video display.

"Lonyu Lyuf Raika Febdak?" Lafiel inquired.

"Lafiel, is that you?"

"Jinto!" The emotion in Lafiel's voice surprised everyone, including herself. "Are you okay?"

"Mostly, yes. You?"

"Listen up. The baron might be on his way over there."

"What? Why?"

"To kill you."

"Jeez, you really know how to brighten my day. Well, what should I do? There aren't any weapons here."

"Can you escape somehow?" she asked.

"Sure, but according to the old man, we'd probably die in the process."

"Knowing you, he's probably right."

"You're a real confidence-booster, Lafiel. You know, we might be able to escape, if you could come pick us up in the Pelia."

"How?"

"There's a Bes in here."

Lafiel was about to ask for more details when Alusa interrupted. "Your Highness the Princess, I've pinpointed the baron's whereabouts. He's in the Shirsh Belysegar!"

"Did you hear that, Jinto? The baron is in the control room. I guess he's got bigger fish to fry than you."

"That bastard!" Jinto joked.

Suddenly, the wall displays went dark and the letters, numbers, and pictures ceased their mathematical dance.

"What was that?" Lafiel asked.

Without answering, Alusa frantically tapped at her control console. After a few seconds, she looked up. "They're trying to kill our system functions, Feia. It should be okay though, because I locked out one part of the Eifu input. So we can keep operating from here; we just can't duplicate the functions of the control room."

"What capabilities did we lose?"

"Remote control of the Joth and Sov Vekekar, observation and surveillance of star system satellites, communications within the star system . . ."

"Do we at least have control of arrival and departure at the dock?"

Timidly, Alusa shook her head.

"Fine. We'll manage." Lafiel knew that a military vessel leaving port didn't *require* cooperation from Air Traffic Control (Belysega). "I'm going to the Pelia."

"You can count on us to hold down the fort," Seelnay said. "And don't worry, Kufaspia is the only one of us with a weapon."

"Why is that?"

"She's the Lyuf's favorite," Seelnay cringed, "because she's his lover and—"

"Got it," Lafiel interrupted. Time was valuable. She spoke into the comms device: "Jinto, I'm going now."

"I'll be waiting," he said with a laugh.

Lafiel terminated the communication.

"Feia Lartneir, I've opened all the doors to the arrival and departure hall," Alusa announced smartly.

"Thanks." Lafiel turned to Greida. "What if I want to communicate with Jinto from inside the Pelia? Can you connect the Luode to the common circuit?"

Greida paused to consider this. "No. We'd have to rewire it. It wouldn't be difficult, but it would take too long."

"So there's nothing we could do?" Lafiel asked impatiently.

"We could try to get a Luode into the retirement section," Alusa proposed.

"Can we do that?"

"The Shirsh Spaurthot Mata!" Seelnay squealed.

"What's that?"

"The delivery room. There's a food transport corridor we use to stock Lonyu Lyuf Raika's fridge," Seelnay explained. "I have full access to that area, so we'll use that corridor to deliver a comms device."

"Great. Now, anybody have a spare comms device?"

"How about my Kreuno?" Seelnay proposed.

"Thanks. What's the contact number?"

Using her own computer wristband, Lafiel saved Seelnay's contact digits for later.

"Okay, I'm going to the Shirsh Spaurthot Mata. Alusa, you should stay here, because that's what you do best." Seelnay seemed to have forgotten Greida.

Anticipating an overly emotional reaction, Lafiel told Seelnay to be careful. As if on cue, Seelnay spewed histrionic gratitude.

Lafiel's mind started to wander, wondering what Jinto was doing. "I'm going now," Lafiel said. "Take care of things."

"Feia Lartneir, wait!" Seelnay interrupted her own tearful speech. She ran up to Lafiel, holding out the Klanyu. "Please, take this. Lonyu Jarluker Dreur might need a weapon."

"What about you?"

"I have Kufaspia's Ribwasia."

"Very well." Lafiel accepted the Klanyu, stashing it in her decorative sash (Kutaroev) before bolting from the room.

2 Abh Style (Bal Gelsas)

Stupid, stupid, stupid!

The baron's mind swirled a million miles an hour. *Why wasn't I more careful? How very un-Abh-like of me!*

He should have stuck to his first instincts: either ensure the visitors' immediate departure or detain them forcibly.

He thought of the traitorous Gosuk. He couldn't believe how quickly they'd changed allegiance as soon as the Lartnier showed up. The Gosuk that he'd imagined were diamonds (Latekrirl) turned out to be nothing but hollow glass spheres. *Why are they such sticklers for the Frybar? Don't they know the Empire is bound to abandon this territory?*

Well, at least he had the loyalty of the four Gosuk with him in the Shirsh Belysegar. The baron growled. "You guys aren't crazy, right?"

"Loyalty-wise?" Control Room Chief Officer (Alm Belysega) Fegdakupe Muiniish inquired.

"Yes!"

"Of course not," Muiniish proclaimed.

"There's no need to even ask us that," added Fegdakupe Belsa, the commanding officer of the makeshift battle group.

"I see. You are true vassals. You will follow me, even against the princess?"

"We'd stand by you, even if she were Spunej Erumita!" Belsa declared.

The baron silently assessed Belsa's statement. *Why should I trust you?* He quickly compiled a mental list of trustworthy Gosuk. The list was short.

I need to show them who's boss. Then, even the defectors will once again pledge allegiance to me!

"Banzorl Garyuk here, calling all Gosuk," Alusa's voice rang out through the room; it was a mansion-wide broadcast. "Currently, there is a dispute within the Lyumex. I repeat: there is an erupting conflict. Our lord, Lonyu Lyum Febdak, has unlawfully confined Feia Lartneir's Pelia during a military mission. Feia Lartneir wishes to leave the Lyumex immediately with her companion, Lonyu Jarluker Dreur Haider."

"Datykril!" the baron yelled, in a vain attempt to dial into the Eifu through his computer wristband.

An error message told him it was impossible to connect.

"But I'm the master of this house!" he screamed.

"Input-output with a regular Luode is an impossible function," the wristband explained. "Please use an established Soteyua."

"For crying out loud!" The baron could not believe this. It was those good-for-nothing, traitorous Gosuk. He turned to Muiniish. "Fire up a computer terminal. Now!"

Alusa continued her speech. "Consequently, we must cooperate with Her Highness the Princess. Feia has promised that those who help will be appointed as vassals of Lartei Kryb. That means we can go to the Imperial capital, Lakfakalle!"

"Nonsense!" the baron cried. "Don't believe it. The Lartei can't take Gosuk so easily. They just can't. Muiniish, is that thing running yet?"

"It's no good," Muiniish said, shrugging. "I can't connect either."

"Damn it!" The baron pointed to Belsa and the other women behind her. "All of you come with me. We'll use another Soteyua. Muiniish, you stay here and figure out how to do your damn job!"

"Wait!" Muiniish cried. "There's an intruder in the Pelia!"

The baron stopped dead in his tracks. "Are you sure?"

Muiniish nodded. Klowal knew his options were limited and undesirable if the Pelia took flight.

While she prepared the Pelia for departure, Lafiel tried to make sense of the announcement she'd just heard. She couldn't tell if it was Alusa or Seelnay, but whoever it was had misunderstood; Lafiel didn't have the authority to choose anybody as a Lartei Kryb Gosuk. She thought she'd made that clear, but apparently she hadn't. Normally, she didn't care if people thought she was dishonest, but she didn't want them to think so for a silly misunderstanding.

Oh well, she thought, *Father always said that no matter what Fasanzoerl say, people hear what they want.*

Shrugging it off, Lafiel slid into the pilot's seat and jacked her control tiara's connector cables (Alpha Kiseg) to the steering mechanism. Her spatial sense (Frokaj) kicked in, and she could sense the laughably-small world beneath her.

Using her computer wristband, Lafiel transferred an internal map of the Lyumex to the Pelia's computer crystal. Using the location of the dock as a point of reference, she incorporated the map into her Frokaj. Once that was accomplished, she instinctively knew where all the walls of the structure were.

While sliding her arm into the ship's control glove (Gooheik), Lafiel initiated the emergency detachment procedure. Numbers and words flitted across the main display screen at illegible speeds until the words "No Abnormalities" (Gosnoh) appeared in large, bold print.

The only setback, as far as Lafiel saw it, was that the vessel's landing legs were firmly locked to the dock. Only the Belysega Lyumusko could enter the command to release the legs.

Somehow, Lafiel thought, *I don't think she'll grant me clearance for takeoff.*

Without a second thought, Lafiel closed the hatch (Lo Yadobel) and fired up the low-temperature jet propulsion system. The landing legs snapped right off. As a result, her next landing would probably be a bit bumpy, but that was a concession Lafiel had to make.

Expanding her spatial sense to a ten-Sedaj radius, Lafiel mentally investigated the space around her. There was a fuel tank asteroid (Sov Vekekar) close by.

It was a gamble though; the Lyuf did say the nearest fuel tanks were all empty. There was no good reason for Lafiel to believe him, however. She was sure it was just one of the many lies he'd told to keep them there.

There wasn't any way to get fuel directly at the pier without the controller's cooperation, but Lafiel could do it herself at a Sov Vekekar. It would be difficult, but she was confident of her school (Kenru) training.

The only question is — should I gas up now or rescue Jinto first?

Lafiel tried punching Seelnay's Kreuno number into her own computer wristband.

"It is not installed," the machine said.

Well, I guess he's not ready for me yet. The fuel tank it is!

When Lafiel directed the Pelia toward the fuel tank asteroid, it seemed to run away, as if engaging her in a game of space-tag.

Run if you want, Lafiel thought, *but I'm really good at being "It."*

The Pelia's acceleration efficiency was far superior to that of the asteroid. It looked like it was going to be a short chase. But then, before she could close much of the gap, the asteroid exploded.

A rush of charged particles splattered against the front of her ship.

Lafiel quickly multiplied the range of her Frokaj a hundredfold. All the Sov Vekekar around the fixed star Febdash were exploding!

And now there was something . . . it looked like a cylindrical craft, exiting the Bidaut. As soon as it was a safe distance from the Garish, it exploded.

Well done, Lyuf Febdak, Lafiel mentally applauded her opponent, *destroying all the antimatter fuel in true Abh style.*

Her response, Lafiel decided, would have to be equally brutal. After she rescued Jinto, she would, without question, have to kill the baron. From the moment Lafiel met the Lyuf, there was something unsettling about the proportion of his head to his shoulders. Someone unaccustomed to Abh beauty probably wouldn't have even noticed, but the baron's overly large cranium bothered Lafiel enough that she relished the opportunity to relieve his neck and shoulders of their burden.

Pulling a one-eighty in the Pelia, Lafiel tightened the range of her Frokaj.

Heading back to the Lyumex, she searched for the wing in which Jinto was imprisoned. Although there was no Baud noted on the internal map, Lafiel could still tell where it was. She fired the low-temperature propulsion jets.

Suddenly, Lafiel's computer wristband beeped the glorious signal of an incoming communication.

"Lafiel!" Jinto yelled into the Kreuno he'd just pulled out of a refrigerator.

"Jinto," Lafiel said, calming him. "Listen up. I can't dock, or make any kind of normal landing."

Pulse quickening, Jinto asked her what that meant.

"Well, basically . . ." Lafiel began. "You got any Gono in there? Pressurized suits would really come in handy."

"Oh man," Jinto groaned. "No, no Gono in here."

"I see. I suppose you'll just have to swim through the vacuum, then," Lafiel said cheerfully. "Just get as close as possible to the ship. When I give the signal, open the Baud and I'll dangle a Kareug from the airlock."

"Great, thanks," Jinto remarked flatly. Since the atmosphere was thick in this section, it would probably take a long time for it all to leak out. So, if everything went smoothly, for the most part, Jinto's ascent to the ship would be comparable to breathing the thin air on a really tall mountaintop. However, given his track record, Jinto did not expect everything to go smoothly.

"You know," remarked the old man, "I'm looking forward to the chance to bask in the glory of your girlfriend, Feia Lartneir."

"I told you, she's *not* my girlfriend," Jinto replied quickly. "But I'll bet she'll be equally pleased to meet you, sir."

"It'll just remind me how terribly old I am. Oh well. I'll go get ready now."

Fighting the mansion's artificial gravity, Lafiel kept a steady distance between the Lyumex and the Pelia.

The circular door loomed beneath the ship, less than a hundred Daj away.

Opening the Yadobel's hatch, she let out the Kareug. The Pelia's ladder was originally designed for rescuing hapless souls drifting through space, so Lafiel could control it remotely.

As the artificial gravity took hold of the ladder, it reached almost to the Baud.

"Jinto," Lafiel spoke into her Kreuno. "Everything's in place on my end."

"Ours too." Jinto sounded nervous.

"Good. If you step away from the Baud, I should be able to shoot the Kareug in."

"Sounds like a plan."

"Once you and Lyuf Raika have a grip on the ladder, I'll pull you in. Hopefully, there will still be some atmosphere in there."

"Pull fast, okay?"

"The Pelia's hovering over Lonyu Lyuf Raika's retirement section," Muiniish stated.

Infuriated, the baron wrung his hands. "Doesn't she know when to quit?"

Klowal was running out of ideas. He'd already imprisoned Lafiel's friend, had his goon squad threaten

Lafiel with guns, and blew up all the Sov Vekekar—
theoretically stranding her.

*I really hope she throws in the towel before I'm forced to kill
her*, he thought. *That's one thing I don't really want to do.*

Unfortunately, his options were growing fewer by the
minute. The whole situation was quite out of hand. Unable
to swallow his immense pride, the baron prepared to make
himself an enemy of the Frybar.

"Everybody, get your weapons and follow me," the
Lyuf commanded, ready for a fight.

Similar in appearance to huge beetles, mechanical cleaners
(Knaik Kowikia) crawled across the ceiling. Their long,
multipurpose limbs latched onto the Baud's emergency
release handle.

"Ready?" the Lyuf Raika verified.

Profusely sweaty, Jinto exhaled. "As I'll ever be."

"Excellent." The old man looked up to the Onhokia.
"Okay, guys. Twist!"

Jinto never even saw the machines move. A white
mist descended in the room, signaling the commencement
of sudden depressurization. Abrupt pressure changes
assaulted Jinto's ears, causing severe ringing.

Like an oddly shaped meteor, the rope ladder shot
out of the sky, crashing into the pond. Jinto ran for the
Kareug, with the surprisingly nimble old man right on
his heels.

While Jinto squirreled half of his body in between
rungs on the rope ladder, the old man secured himself. The
former baron gave Jinto a thumbs-up.

Even though the temperature hadn't changed, the
pond started to boil.

"Okay, Lafiel," Jinto squeaked. The thin atmosphere was really straining his vocal cords. "Pulls us in!"

Immediately, the ladder lurched upward. The Kareug ascended with frustrating slowness. But since it was pulling Jinto away from impending doom, he couldn't really object. Although collision with the ceiling seemed imminent, Jinto and the old man were able to avoid it by contorting their bodies in ways that would please a circus crowd.

As the two men got sucked through the Baud into normal space (Dath), Jinto could feel the air getting thinner by the second. As a child, Jinto had once found delight jumping on a bellows to see how fast he could squeeze the air out. Now, he understood how the bellows felt.

Before they could even fully understand or appreciate the rare experience, Jinto and the old man entered the Pelia's Yadobel. Unfortunately for them, the atmosphere was rapidly escaping out of the airlock.

Jinto tried to shout to Lafiel, but couldn't find the breath. Regardless, the air was too thin to transmit a vibrating sound wave anyway.

Hanging onto the airlock's ceiling, he stared at the wide-open hatch, terrified.

After a seemingly infinite period of time (which was actually less than one second), the Lo slammed shut. Four vents immediately spewed atmosphere into the room, creating a turbulent eddy of lifesaving air.

Ears still ringing, Jinto greedily gulped it in. His heart, which was beating abnormally fast, slowly returned to normal. Relief settled over him, as he realized that they'd made it.

Untangling himself from the rope ladder, Jinto dropped to the floor. The atmosphere was still thin, but at that point, he wasn't picky. He helped Lyuf Raika down from the Kareug.

Both men slumped against the wall, sucking in huge, well-deserved breaths. The old man looked unsettled, but he kept quiet.

Eventually, a blue light indicated that the atmosphere had returned to normal, and the door to the cockpit (Shirsh Sediar) opened.

Although he hoped to commemorate their reunion with a powerful and gripping speech, Jinto could only think that it was the first time he'd seen Lafiel in a long robe (Daush). A silver bird on the malachite-colored sash demanded his attention.

"Someone's all dressed up," Jinto noted. "You look good!

Visions of the princess grabbing him in an emotional embrace danced through his head. Her voice brought him back to reality.

"Are you hurt?" She still hadn't moved.

"As you can see, we're just fine."

"Good. You're the most important cargo I've got, so I'd be really annoyed if you got hurt."

"See," Jinto whispered into the old man's ear, "I told you she's not my girlfriend."

With eleven trustworthy Gosuk in tow, Lyuf Febdak strode briskly toward the arrival and departure hall. Following directly in his footsteps, Kufaspia finished applying a bandage to her injured hand.

Just as Kufaspia finished dressing the wound, the baron suddenly stopped. He inhaled sharply several times. Something seemed wrong.

"What's the matter, my lord?" Belsa asked.

"Can't you feel it? The air is thin."

Eleven Gosuk inhaled simultaneously before dizzily nodding confirmation.

"Damn. I'll bet I know why!" exclaimed the baron. He dialed the household room's comms device on his Kreuno. "Traitorous dogs, do you read me?"

"Yes . . . Fal Lonyu. We—"

"Greida?!" the baron shouted. "Don't you 'Fal Lonyu' me!"

She said nothing for a moment. "Sorry."

"Yeah, whatever. Has the retirement section lost pressure?"

"Yes."

"Are you taking the appropriate countermeasures?"

"Yes, Fal—er, Lonyu Lyum. I've closed all the atmosphere circulation ducts."

"That's it? What about the garbage processing system?"

"Oh no!" Greida shrieked. "I totally forgot!"

"Frankly, I'm not surprised. Well, if you're all still crammed in the Banzorl Garyuk, be careful; the atmosphere's probably leaking."

"I'm so sorry."

"Don't apologize, just fix it."

"I can't do it from here. The garbage processing system can't close itself."

"Onyu!" the baron snapped. "It's not that difficult. Either close it by hand or dispatch the mansion's external maintenance crew. I don't care what you do, as long as you do something now!"

The baron punctuated this command by hanging up on Greida.

It's so hard to find good help these days, the baron thought. *If they're not mutinous, they're totally incompetent.*

Honestly! They can't treat this like a minor maintenance issue when it could kill us all.

"They're going to screw it up even more," the baron said to the eleven Gosuk behind him. "I just know it. We'd better find some Gono and suit up before they suffocate us all."

The Lyuf's mind turned to his father, who'd probably escaped with the lander. If that old man got his hands on a computer terminal, the baron knew it could make the situation even more complicated.

Uh-oh, the baron realized. *There are terminals on the Pelia.* If they performed data concatenation (Lonjhoth Rirrag) with the Pelia's Datykril and the mansion's Eifu, then those terminals would function the same as the ones inside the mansion.

"You guys keep going. If you see Feia Lartneir, restrain her by any means necessary. Got it?"

"You're not coming with us?" Belsa quivered.

"No," he answered gravely. "I'm going out."

There was a free-for-all in the household rooms. Back from the Shirsh Spaurthot Mata, Seelnay and Alusa engaged Sesume in an epic debate about whether it was nobler to be loyal to the baron or the Empire. Unladylike words and names flew back and forth.

Adding to the cacophony, the comms device beeped with incessant connection requests; although most of the mansion's Gosuk were too frightened to leave their rooms once all hell broke loose, they still wanted to keep abreast of the situation.

While most of the Gosuk had completely abandoned their duties, Greida continued to work. Compensating for the others' lack of industriousness, she moved at double speed. Adding to her woes, she couldn't use at least half of her computer terminal's functions. That was her excuse for overlooking the mansion's depressurization.

The Datykril should have warned us, Greida reasoned. Evidently, when Alusa blocked the baron from using his crystal to interfere, she'd erroneously shut down too many functions. Alusa was prone to get excited and overdo things.

"Everyone, listen up!" Greida rose from her seat.

"Not now," Seelnay said, without even turning to look, "we're busy!"

"Well, I'm busier!" Greida roared.

No one had ever heard Greida yell like that before. Mouths agape, the five women in the room awaited Greida's next words.

"Quit bickering and shut off that damn Luode!"

"Yes, ma'am!" Alusa switched off the comms device, and all was quiet.

Still glaring fiercely, Greida began an internal broadcast. "This is Banzorl Garyuk. The mansion is losing air pressure. Complete loss of atmosphere is imminent. Do not use the garbage disposal chutes. If you see an open chute, close it and make sure it is sealed with Dib."

"Losing pressure?" Seelnay's eyes ballooned.

"Yes. Feia Lartneir opened the Baud in the retirement section, and apparently forgot to close it. Although it theoretically shouldn't affect the rest of the mansion, our atmosphere is leaking through the garbage chutes."

"But everything feels okay to me."

"Banzorl Garyuk is still airtight."

"Told you!" Lulune chirped triumphantly. "Feia Lartneir doesn't care about us. We must be loyal and stand by Fal Lonyu!"

"Shut up!" Greida slapped her Kuro. "It's necessary to do some external mansion work to correct this problem. Seelnay, you have your vacuum work license, right?"

"Of course. What do you want me to do?"

"Isn't it obvious? Go close the Baud and reseal it!"

"Oh, right." Seelnay nodded. "I won't be able to do it alone."

"Okay. The rest of you go with her," Greida ordered.

"But I'm just a Partia," Sesume protested. "I certainly don't have a vacuum work license. Besides, I can't work with that—"

"Stop it!" Greida pounded the console again. "There's no time to be petty. No excuses! I don't care if you have a license or not. Just get it done!"

"She's right," Seelnay agreed. "You'll have to work with me, unless you'd prefer us all to die."

Heads hanging, the four Gosuk obeyed. Sesume stopped in the door to get the last word. "Aren't you coming, Greida?"

"I'm needed here," Greida said, puffing out her chest. "I'm the Alm Goneudo."

For a moment, Sesume looked as if she might say something nasty, but she thought better of it and followed Seelnay out of the room.

Alusa remained in the room, next to her regular work station.

"I can handle it in here, Alusa. You should go too. They'll need all the hands they can get."

Hesitantly, Alusa acquiesced—Greida was her superior officer. Alone at last, Greida resumed working.

Although the title Household Rooms Chief Officer sounded impressive, Greida didn't usually get the respect she deserved in Lyumusko Febdak. She was an essential part of the mansion's day-to-day operations, but didn't have nearly as much power as the prettier Gosuk, such as the clothier (Daushasairl) and the bedroom duty official (Diafsairl), who also slept with the baron. It was ridiculous; those girls weren't even fluent in Baronh!

After spending so much time in Lyumusko Febdak, Greida had started to forget why she'd left her sandy homeworld in the first place. True, she had no family and no friends there, but she didn't have any at the baron's mansion, either. Ever since she'd become an Imperial Citizen (Lef), she'd begun to grow more and more disenchanted with life.

But now she'd found something else she enjoyed: bossing other people around. It was fun, and she appeared to have a real knack for it.

And it was important for someone to give orders. At this point, they couldn't plausibly sit around and wait for instructions. Feia Lartneir was too busy trying to escape, and the baron seemed to be completely off his rocker.

Greida had no interest in the quarrel between the princess and the baron. She didn't know who would win, let alone who was right. Regardless of the outcome, Greida knew it was vital to keep the household running, and that she was the only one qualified to shoulder that responsibility.

Reaching for the comms device, Greida prepared to address all the Gosuk who'd abandoned their duties.

"Just checking, Lyuf Raika," Lafiel probed, "but you're on our side, right?" As she spoke, her hand instinctively inched toward her laser pistol.

"His Excellency is our ally," Jinto assured.

"Feia Lartneir," Lyuf Raika Febdak hailed. "If the damn fool also known as my son caused you any trouble, I'll see to it that he's punished accordingly."

Gripping the gun, Lafiel said, "Thanks, but I can kill him myself."

"Feia," the old man pleaded, "isn't that a bit extreme?"

"He interfered with a Labule mission. He's lucky I won't torture him." The two men stared at her. "The Lyuf blew up all the Sov Vekekar!"

"Ah." Jinto contemplated this. "That might be a problem."

"Can't you be serious for once, Jinto?" Lafiel raged. "You're not mad enough."

"I'm tired, Lafiel. Let me take a nap and I'll get angry later, okay?"

"Onyu!"

"Now, now, Feia," Lyuf Raika interceded. "If it's just a matter of fuel, I'm sure we can figure something out."

"How?" Lafiel snapped.

"Has my son destroyed the Joth as well?"

Lafiel shook her head. "I don't think so. As far as I know, they're still fine."

"Then we should be able to scare up some Baish at the factories. Not enough to fly a Star Force battleship or anything, but it'll be enough to power this little thing."

"That would work," Lafiel pointed out, "if the control room weren't under the baron's authority. Without a compliant Belysega, there's nothing we can do."

"Just leave that part to me." The old man winked.

"Lonyu Lyuf Raika designed this whole Garish," Jinto explained. "It should be easy for him to hijack its Datykril." Jinto turned to the old man. "Right?"

"In theory. No harm trying, right?"

"Okay," Lafiel agreed.

"If it works out, Feia," the old man pleaded, "do you think you could you leave my worthless child's punishment to me?"

"I'm not sure I like that condition."

"Please? I'd really prefer if you didn't kill him."

"Fine," Lafiel relented. While she couldn't control her own rage against the baron, Abh societal ethics suggested it was improper to interfere with other families' problems. If the Febdash family wanted to sort its own issues out, then Lafiel wouldn't interfere. "But I won't hesitate to kill the Lyuf if he gets in our way again."

The baron nodded solemnly. "Understandable. Now, can you lend me a Luode? I can't hack into the Eifu without one."

"Yes. Come into the cockpit," Lafiel invited.

Sliding into the pilot's seat, Lafiel patted the copilot's chair. Seeing his chair usurped, Jinto hovered petulantly behind them.

"Wow, these things sure have changed since my day," the former baron mumbled as he poked at the computer terminal. "I don't think I even know how to turn it on."

"The way you were talking earlier, it sounded like you invented these!" Jinto exclaimed.

Lafiel began to worry that their only hopes rested on this inept old man.

"Don't worry, Faneb! I won't even need to operate the Soteyua."

"Then why are you making such a big deal about it?"

"Excuse me for being interested! I am an engineer, you know. Okay, Feia, show me how this Soteyua works, please."

"Me? I have to fly the ship."

"Just long enough for me to see it in action. The interface is a bit different, but it's fundamentally the same as the old ones, so I'll learn really quickly."

The old man had Lafiel set the Luode's wavelength to some frequency he pulled out of his memory. Immediately, he began speaking a foreign language.

"What are you doing now?" Lafiel asked warily.

Ignoring her, Lyuf Raika continued jabbering at the machine. Rolling her eyes, Lafiel looked to Jinto for an explanation. Jinto pretended not to notice.

The Lyumex's main computer (Opdatykril) was too inundated with cross-purposed orders to do much, except to determine that the mansion was in a complete state of chaos.

A glut of non-prioritized messages bogged down the comms circuits. At the rate the commands were coming in, the machine simply could not do anything except count the messages as they piled up. Since the humans in the house had restricted its inputs, all the computer could do was pretend to be dumb.

Doubtless, the machine would be relieved if it were capable of emotions, safe in the knowledge that there were no circumstances in which the machine could devolve into a state of disorder as profound as the humans'.

Then, without warning, a message arose from the computer's control layer (Faroll Sok) to execute one of the computer's older programs, which had been dormant for some time. The program issued the highest priority command known to the computer, effectively instructing the Opdatykril to ignore everything else.

Thus, the computer was reborn with a new set of tasks; chaos was no longer on its agenda.

First, the Opdatykril performed Lonjhoth Rirrag with a computer crystal that was outside the mansion. It was a brand new Datykril that the main computer did not recognize, transmitting information at an extremely slow rate from a few Wesdaj away. Although it was slow, the new computer crystal was able to send a command that disconnected the main computer from all the others in the house.

The new Datykril then issued a few commands. First, it instructed the computer to ignore any requests to open any of the mansion's doors. Next, it requested all the available information about the antimatter fuel factories. It asked about Joth Lokeutona, an antimatter fuel factory relatively close to the mansion. The factory had a lot of fuel, nearly enough to fill a whole Sov Vekekar.

After sending the new user the Joth's orbital data, the main computer, as per its instructions, linked the new user's Datykril to the computer crystal of the antimatter fuel factory. Finally, the external Datykril requested a report of all the Lyuf's actions in the last hour.

The Opdatykril sent the message that the master of the house had left.

Now, Jinto realized, *I really am just cargo.*

Once the Pelia began its acceleration, Jinto slumped by the wall separating the Yadobel from the cockpit. At that point, there was nothing he could do. Lafiel was busy flying the ship, and the Lyuf Raika (who had apparently already bridged his twenty-year technology gap) operated the Soteyua. Neither gave any indication of needing help, and they wouldn't ask Jinto even if they did.

Jinto squirmed, realizing that he'd spent much of his life feeling equally out of place. If it was his destiny to feel permanently useless, then it was probably easier to accept it than to wage a futile battle against fate that would render him even more despondent.

"Feia," the old man shattered the silence. "This could get complicated."

"Why do you say that?"

"It appears my son is in a Ponyu."

"Is that ship armed?"

The former baron shrugged. "Beats me. I haven't been in charge of the Ribeun for some time now." He looked at the computer. "Oh. That's right. Hang on, I'll try to get some information from this computer thingamabob."

Staring intently at the display screen, Lyuf Raika tapped at the terminal's Kuro.

Wanting to get in on the action, Jinto stood up between the pilot and copilot chairs. "How does it look?"

"Like one of these," the baron said, pointing at some ship specifications on his display screen. "It's a Dakteif-built Segunow nine-forty-seven class. Equipped with two Lengarf-forty warship Klanyu."

"Can we control them from here?" inquired Lafiel.

"I'm afraid not. The little stinker took his ship's Datykril off the Eifu."

"I see." Lafiel stared at the screen, contemplating the specs of the Segunow. "Lyuf Raika, we may have to kill your son after all."

It was impossible to read the expression that passed over the old man's face, and it was gone before anyone could give it too much thought. He sighed and said, "Yes, I suppose it can't be helped."

"But," Jinto cut in, "this Pelia isn't even armed, is it?"

"No, it's not."

"So . . ." sputtered Jinto, unable to follow Abh logic. If the baron was armed and they weren't, shouldn't they be more worried about him killing them? "Why are you so cocky about it?"

"Cocky?" Lafiel repeated, as if she had never heard the word before.

"It's an Abh thing, Faneb," Lyuf Raika interjected. "Feia doesn't necessarily believe she'll win; she just doesn't waste time imagining her own demise."

"That's . . ." Once again, Jinto's thought disintegrated on its way out of his mouth.

Luckily the former baron was there to interpret. "Lonyu Jarluker Dreur misunderstood. He thought Your Highness hadn't considered the possibility that this vessel will be destroyed."

"Do you think I'm stupid?" Lafiel glared at Jinto. "We barely have a ten percent chance of winning. I know that much."

Jinto's estimation had been closer to zero percent, so he felt slightly encouraged to hear that figure. However, the odds were still greatly stacked against them. "And you're still willing to fight?"

"What other options do we have?"

"This, too, is typical Abh behavior," the old man commented. "They'll take even the slimmest chance over surrender, which is simply not an option."

"Do you object, Lyuf Raika?" Lafiel asked.

"Far from it, Feia. I'm an Abh too, you know." He winked. "I know when I have to fight."

"Jinto? Any objections?"

"I'm merely the cargo." Jinto shrugged. "Just do your best to deliver me in one piece, okay?"

Lyumusko Febdak had four interstellar cruise ships. One was a transport ship (Kasorvia) that shuttled gases to and from the little planet. Its speed was equivalent to that of a turtle, and the baron hated it.

Two of the territory's ships were ferries that carried maintenance personnel to and from the Joth and Sov Vekekar. The last ship was the baron's personal vessel, which unlike the other three ships, had Abh-style steering equipment. This was also the only armed ship in the territory. The baron called it *Lady Febdash* (Loj Febdak).

The baron located the Pelia with his Frokaj; the little ship was on its way toward the eleventh antimatter fuel factory. Unlike the Sov Vekekar, the Joth couldn't be remotely detonated. Even if he tried to destabilize the Baish, the factory's Datykril would correct the mistake.

Normally, the baron would be able to regulate the flow of fuel. That had changed now that the old man was helping them, though.

The Lyuf picked up the Luode. "Control room, can you hear me?"

"Yes; this is Muiniish in the Shirsh Belysegar."

"Do we still have remote control of Joth Lokeutona?"

"Well, th-that's . . ." Muiniish stuttered. "For some reason, the control room's functions are locked. We can't get control. I have no idea how Feia Lartneir did this."

The baron hung up his comms device quite rudely. Just as he suspected, his father was aboard the Pelia, abetting the enemy. *Unbelievable!*

To resent the codger, the baron knew, would be naïve. A bitter smile spread across his face. He increased his beloved ship's acceleration.

Being an Abh himself, the baron knew the Lartneir wouldn't entertain negotiations at this stage. It was far too late for that. Soon enough, he would have to turn Feia's Pelia into space dust.

The Lyuf knew the Pelia contained only a little girl posing as a Bene Lodair; an old, potentially senile, shipbuilding engineer (Fazia Har); and a lander brat with no military training at all.

The baron, on the other hand, had served as an honorable Deca-Commander (Lowas), even if it had only been in the reserves. While he had no actual battle experience, he'd spent an enormous amount of time in mock battles.

On top of that, his ship was superior to theirs. Simply put, there was no reason for him to lose.

The distance between the ships shrank rapidly. Finally, the baron was within firing range. In a couple seconds he would be close enough to deliver a fatal shot. Prepared to unleash the devastating laser beams (Klanraj), the baron tightened his grip on the trigger.

"Goodbye, Father," the baron muttered, unaware of the tears instinctively forming in his eyes.

Sensing danger, the hairs on Lafiel's neck stood up.

Although they rarely showed it, the Abh feared death as much as anyone else. Adding to her fright, Lafiel had two other people's lives in her hands. The baron's vessel was closing in on them and would soon be within critical distance.

Contorting her fingers inside the control glove, Lafiel fired the altitude control jets from eight different directions, changing the Pelia's course.

Here it comes!

The Pelia narrowly avoided two Klanraj—one even grazed the ship. Lafiel quickly changed course again.

Another laser beam. Another near-miss.

Since Klanraj traveled at the speed of light, they would be impossible to avoid if the baron got off a good shot. It was simply a battle of intuition; who would make the best guess of the other's next maneuver? Whose side would luck take?

Fortunately, for the time being, luck was on Lafiel's side. However, she didn't know how long that would last. She shut her eyes, tuning out everything but her Frokaj.

A little more. Just a little closer.

Patiently awaiting an opportunity, Lafiel dodged unyielding Klanraj. She knew she would only get one chance, and if she missed it, that would be that. Her heart seemed to be stuck in her throat—a thoroughly uncomfortable feeling. She knew they were toast if even one of the lasers hit them.

"Here we go!"

Manipulating the Gooheik like a pro, Lafiel killed the main engine and fired the reverse thrust jets at full throttle simultaneously.

Maximum deceleration resulted.

The Pelia's tail shot diagonally across the Lyuf's ship. Right before it entered the baron's crosshairs, Lafiel gunned the main engine (Opsei).

With his spacial sense, the baron detected a lump of gas moving toward his ship. The clump of fog flew straight at the front end of his spacecraft like a spear made of gas.

What the hell is she doing?

Propulsion exhaust wouldn't harm his ship; it was thin and not very hot.

It seemed like a meaningless gesture. The lump of gas would definitely shield the Pelia from Klanraj for a few brief seconds, but it would disperse as soon as he passed through it, and then he would catch them again quickly.

Sensing there was no way to avoid the miasma, the baron decided to rocket through it the way a little boy thrusts his arm through a waterfall. The baron gesticulated the Gooheik for full acceleration into the mist.

As he crossed the propulsion exhaust, the *Loj Febdak's* hull got white-hot and the whole ship's interior filled with a raging radioactive storm. Scorching heat instantly blinded the baron.

A split second after the incredible pain gripped him, the Lyuf understood his mistake. The Abh had an expression for being excessively wasteful: *Using Baish for propulsion*. The desperate Lartneir had done just that, using Baish's incredibly inefficient thrust to create antimatter exhaust that would substitute for a proton cannon.

"Gaaaahhh!" the baron shouted, blood gushing from his mouth.

For the remaining moments of his life, the baron's heart was filled with admiration for Lafiel.

Watching the *Loj Febdak* careen out of the star system at top speed, Lafiel directed the Pelia toward the eleventh Joth. Since she'd used most of the Pelia's propellant (Biiz) in her battle with the baron, she would have to move slowly toward the fuel factory.

"Is it over?" Jinto asked, finally breathing.

"Yes, it's over." Lafiel looked up at Jinto. During the battle, he must have hit something, because his eye was starting to swell up.

"Did you kill the Lyuf?"

"Yes, I did." Lafiel sighed. She was exhausted. Her voiced seemed to come from someone else. "The Ponyu survived, but there's nobody alive inside it." Lafiel turned to the old man. "Condolences, Lyuf Raika."

"All's fair in war, Feia," the old man acknowledged sadly.

"Condolences? Is that all?" Jinto snapped.

"What's the matter, Jinto?" Lafiel asked, taken aback.

"You just killed somebody and you're acting like it's no big deal!"

"If I didn't kill him, he would have killed us."

"I know! I'm relieved that it turned out the way it did. I really am. But still, don't you think you should feel a little remorse?"

"Why? It's just part of the job," she snapped at Jinto, who seemed to regard her as some kind of monster now. "If I thought I might ever feel an ounce of regret about it, then I never would have done it."

"I mean . . . well . . . in general, it just seems like you should be upset when you kill somebody."

"Would it do any good to get upset?"

"Well, no. But—"

"You're being completely illogical," Lafiel declared.

"I know," Jinto admitted, "but it just seems very cold-blooded, that's all."

"I've never pretended to be a warm person." Lafiel was beginning to roil underneath the surface.

"But . . ."

"It's okay, Faneb." Lyuf Raika interrupted. "You don't have to be upset."

I see. Lafiel understood. *Jinto's not upset at* me. *He's just bent out of shape in general.*

"I know you didn't want to see Feia Lartneir kill someone," said the old man.

"There's no way Jinto could have possibly seen anything from where he was," Lafiel said.

"It was a figure of speech, Feia. He just didn't want to be here when you killed my son."

"Why not?"

"Ask *him,* not me," the old man dodged.

Lafiel looked at Jinto. "Is that true?"

Jinto struggled, muttering a string of nonsense.

Finally, Lafiel cut him off. "We were at war, Jinto. I had to do it."

"I know."

"And you didn't want to see me win the battle?"

"Don't be ridiculous; we'd all be a lot worse off if you'd lost."

"Then what's the problem?"

"I don't know." Jinto hung his head, which was actually a very difficult posture in the cramped space. "I'm sorry I attacked you. You're a Bosnal and shouldn't be ashamed of fighting, especially when it amounts to saving my butt."

Lafiel stared at Jinto, who definitely had not answered her question.

"I forgive you," Lafiel stated, deciding not to press the issue.

"Aw, cute," the former baron cooed, picking up the Luode. "Now that you're through talking, I'm going to resume control of the Skor."

Lyuf Raika was not noticeably fazed by his son's death until, under his breath, the old man exhaled a barely audible, "Idiot son." The statement was imbued with profound sadness.

Easy, Seelnay decided.

When she'd assembled a crew of Gosuk to repair the leak in the air pressure system, they'd expected the Baud to be completely gone. However, the situation was not nearly that grim. The round door was open but still intact, resting upside down on the mansion's ceiling. Burn marks in the area around the door suggested an emergency opening, but the door itself seemed to be in top condition.

Kneeling closer to the Baud, Seelnay confirmed that there were no tears or cracks in it. She stood and faced her makeshift crew.

Seelnay could see the four women's displeasure through their Gono. Although these women wore the pressurized suits twice a year for emergency drills, they'd never expected to need them in the vacuum of space.

Seelnay, on the other hand, worked in vacuum conditions every day.

Three of the women lugged a steel plate, in case the original door was gone or beyond repair. The original Baud would be much more effective, though, so their effort was all for nothing.

Lagging slightly behind them, Alusa arrived with a large, cylindrical tube of Dib.

"You can throw away the steel plate," Seelnay declared.

"Throw it away? Where?" asked Kunyuusa, the baron's clothier.

"Anywhere. Over there's good," Seelnay directed. *We're in the vacuum of space, for crying out loud!*

Seelnay pointed to the Baud. "We're going to use that instead, so you guys will need to bring it over."

Clumsily, the three women dropped the steel plate and walked toward the Baud.

"Come on! We don't have time to waste—atmosphere is still leaking out."

"Thanks to your precious princess," Lulune countered petulantly.

"Don't talk about her like that!" Seelnay snapped.

"Let's just get this done," Kunyuusa pleaded.

"Well, look who's decided to be sensible all of a sudden," Semune quipped.

Incessantly bickering, the three women lifted the Baud and fitted it into place under Seelnay's direction.

"Alusa!" Seelnay called. "Pass the Dib."

"You got it!" Alusa offered her the tube.

Grabbing it, Seelnay pointed its nozzle toward the door. Opening the valve was comparable to igniting a blowtorch, in that it resulted in a sudden, steady emission of white goop. Seelnay plugged the tiny cracks between the door and its hole.

It did the trick, at least for the time being. Ideally, they would weld the door shut—when the retirement section of the mansion returned to normal pressure, the adhesive probably wouldn't hold. Until the situation in the mansion calmed down a little and they had time for proper repairs, they would just have to keep the retirement section at low pressure.

"Can we go now?" Semune asked.

"No," Seelnay refused, even though she didn't need any more help.

"Ridiculous!" Semune exploded, appealing to her allies. "There's nothing more for us to do here! Let's go back and leave the rest to this greasy mechanic!"

"Fine. Do what you want," Seelnay spat.

"We're going," Semune decided. "Vacuum makes me suffocate."

"No kidding."

The three antagonistic women stumbled off, but Alusa remained. A man's voice came through the internal shared frequency.

"Greetings, Gosuk. This is Lyuf Raika Febdak. My son, Atosryua Syun-Atos Lyuf Febdak, has died in battle."

"Lies!" Semune shrieked.

"This will be hard for everyone to accept. Needless to say, he was your lord. And although he wasn't a great son to me, he was still my son. If you want to leave the Skor, I won't stop you. In fact, I am so grateful for your loyalty to my son, I'll do as much as I can to help you. This could be in the form of a lump sum payment, or continued employment. But that's in the future.

"As you've probably already heard, there is an enemy fleet invading Imperial territory, and conflict appears inevitable. I have faith in the Labule, and you should too. But until everything quiets down, I'll need you to accept me as our leader. After that, I will choose and instruct a Golkia to help you all decide the fate of this Skor."

Once the broadcast ended, Seelnay stopped working; the door's hermetic seal was finished. Switching off her wireless receiver, Seelnay stood.

So what if the Lyuf's dead? It's none of my business now— I'm going to be a Gosuk in the Lartei Kryb.

"What do you mean we're not going to make it in time?" Jinto raised his voice from his seat in the Yadobel.

"I meant exactly what I said," Lafiel stated. The Pelia's acceleration was steady at approximately one standard gravity unit (Daemon). "We used almost all our fuel in the battle, so we can't accelerate very quickly. We'll still be a solid six hours away by the time the enemy reaches Sufagnaum."

"How are you not freaking out about this?" Jinto demanded. "I mean, you blow a fuse at every little thing I say."

The outer edges of Lafiel's eyebrows rose in perfect unison.

"See? I speak and you get mad!"

"Does my composure really bother you that much?"

"No."

"Then what's your problem?"

"Well, it's . . ." Jinto wasn't really sure. Why did Lafiel's calmness unnerve him so completely? The more he thought about it, the more he realized it was his problem, not hers.

The fact that nothing fazed Lafiel fed Jinto's preexisting feelings of inferiority. Not only was his unflappable protector younger, this brave soul was also a girl. Jinto's poor ego couldn't take it.

"Okay, you two," the former baron interrupted, saving Jinto from further shame. "Let's think about what to do next. Do you still intend to go to Sufagnaum, Feia?"

"That is my mission," Lafiel proclaimed.

"If you're not careful, you might fly smack into the middle of a battle," the old man imparted. "It's okay with me if you want to stay here. I can't really entertain you properly, but I would certainly be a better host than my son."

"Thanks for the offer." Lafiel stopped, and looked at Jinto like she'd just remembered he was there. "What do you think, Jinto?"

Jinto weighed the options. Since they would arrive after the enemy fleet, it would be pointless to hurry forward. It could even be dangerous if, as the Lyuf Raika suggested, they unwittingly came across a battle. However, logic had no place in Jinto's desire to get the hell out of the Lyumusko as fast as possible.

Abandoning his inner debate, Jinto announced, "The cargo has no opinion."

"So I hear."

"I just don't know," Jinto confessed. "While the cargo has no official stance, I can't help thinking it might be wiser to stay put."

"I see." Lafiel mulled it over. "Lyuf Raika, what do you think?"

"Honestly, I don't have a clue, Feia. I don't want to make the decision, in case it turns out to be the wrong one. Here are my thoughts: If the enemy gets repelled at Sufagnaum, they may come here. In that situation, the Lyumusko cannot protect you, so you probably ought to go to Sufagnaum."

"Then why did you tell us to stay?" Jinto demanded indignantly.

"Calm down, Faneb. I never said you *should* stay, just that I'd gladly accommodate it."

"Well, I'm going," Lafiel decided. "The Abh don't like to wait around for anything. We'd rather go to meet our fate. What are you going to do?"

"What do you mean?" Jinto didn't seem to understand.

"I'm willing to unload the cargo here, in the Lyumusko."

Unexplainable rage surged through Jinto, who took great offense that Lafiel thought he might abandon her. Equally infuriating was the fact that she was willing to let him do it! The emotion registered on his face.

Jinto grumbled. "You will deliver the cargo to Sufagnaum as planned!"

"How about that?" Lafiel marveled. "I speak and you get mad!"

4 Travelers (Lebulaterash)

Fortunately, the Joth had a surplus of Baish. After refueling the Pelia, they cruised toward the Lyumex at full speed.

Lafiel contacted the spaceport as she slowed the ship for docking. It was a slightly bumpy process, because the landing legs were no longer attached to the Pelia. But thanks to her excellent spacial sense and the Datykril, Lafiel didn't even put a dent in the hull.

"I don't know if it's a good idea to go in here, Feia," the old man warned.

"Why not?"

"Accomplices! Some of the Gosuk might be a tad bitter," Lyuf Raika explained. "You killed their master; looks like they're gathered right outside that door with the torches and pitchforks. That's why I've locked us in the spaceport."

"How many are there?"

"Hmm." He tabulated. "Eleven. That's a fifth of the Gosuk. If they're all armed, it would be the most powerful army in the Febdashos."

"You don't want to fight them, do you?" Jinto asked nervously.

"Please," Lafiel dismissed him. "I don't like fighting. It's only a last resort."

For some reason, Jinto imagined her idea of a "last resort" differed from his.

"Don't worry, Faneb," soothed the old man. "Once the Abh start fighting, they finish the job. No negotiations or compromise. That's why they try to avoid it as much as possible."

"Oh yeah?"

"Yes. There is not a single instance in which the Frybar initiated a battle."

"Not true. My star system never even knew the Frybar existed until Labule ships showed up with guns drawn."

"Dreuhynu Haider?"

"Yeah. Didn't you know that, Lonyu Lyuf Raika? Hyde was an independent star system until just seven years ago."

"Oh yes," the old man nodded. "I think I remember reading about you and your family. Regardless, the Empire only makes opponents of interstellar nations. They are great and merciless warriors, but they rarely, rarely, rarely fight on Nahen; they are above it. Literally."

Starting to feel somewhat alienated, Lafiel turned to the old man. "You're an Abh too. Why do you still speak as if you're a lander?"

"Feia," the old man explained respectfully, "I had to *learn* to be an Abh. Right now, this young man, Lonyu Jarluker Dreur, is learning how to be an Abh."

She stiffened. "I don't like you talking about this as if I'm not right here."

The men offered cursory apologies, which Lafiel saw through.

"At any rate, Feia," Lyuf Raika changed the subject, "I suggest you steer this crate toward the Fapyut's personal Bes. There won't be any ambushes brewing there."

"Good idea. Do you have Bynkerlseraj?"

"Yes, the controls completely work. But you can't spare the time it will take me to operate on this terminal. I'll have to restore functionality to the control room. Of course, it's unknown whether they'll follow my instructions," the old man voiced everyone's concern.

Without thinking about it too much more, the former baron picked up the Luode and connected to the Shirsh Belysegar. After a short discussion, it was clear that the Alm Belysega, Muiniish, was on his side, so the former baron began the procedures to give her full control functionality.

"Can we trust her?"

"We can always take away her Bynkerlseraj."

Lafiel signaled approval with the slightest shoulder shrug and picked up the Luode. "Bynkerl Lyumusko Febdak."

"Yes, this is Bynkerl."

"Requesting permission to detach from the dock."

"Okay, I can authorize that. When?"

"Immediately."

"Roger. Releasing dock restraints."

Shortly after, the couplers securing the Pelia to the Bes released their grasp.

Using her Frokaj, Lafiel confirmed the location of the Fapyut's personal dock. She piloted the ship at a crawl along the roof of the Lyumex.

"Bynkerl, come in."

"Yes?"

"Requesting permission to land at the sovereign's exclusive dock."

"Authorizing," Muiniish said after a slight pause. "Do you want guidance?"

"No." This short flight was a piece of cake for a pilot with Frokaj.

In less than a minute, Lafiel parked the ship in the baron's favorite spot. As soon as the Pelia touched down, machines automatically began the process of replenishing their Biiz.

"Well, Feia," Lyuf Raika said, rising. "I must go now, to calm the storm of chaos in the old Garish. Please fly safely, with the knowledge that you're always welcome here."

"Thank you," Lafiel acknowledged. "There were Gosuk, Seelnay and Alusa, who proved their loyalty to the Empire. Would you give them a message for me?"

"Of course," Lyuf Raika assented.

"Thanks." She inserted a memory sheet (Jeish) into her Kreuno.

Then, in a gesture that completely baffled Lafiel, the old man extended his hand to Jinto, whose equally puzzling response was to grasp the hand and pump it up and down a couple times.

"I guess this is it, Faneb. When you get a chance, come visit and tell me all about Druejhe Haider. Maybe I can help you prepare for a lander's life as an Abh."

"Yes. Sounds great."

"If it's possible, come see me before you start having kids." Laughing, the ex-baron nudged Jinto.

Lafiel suddenly remembered what she was supposed to be doing before the lander antics completely distracted her. She brought the Kreuno to her mouth to record her message.

"Greetings, Gosuk Seelnay, Gosuk Alusa, and other Rue Lef whose names I don't know but who also helped me. I, Bene Lodair Abriel Nei Dubrusc Borl Paryun Lafiel, thank you on behalf of the Frybar and myself. At present, I cannot take you with me, but I will come back to repay your goodwill as soon as my situation allows. Please be patient until that time comes. I won't forget this promise."

Finished recording, she took the memory sheet out of the wristband and handed it to Lyuf Leka. "Please show them this."

"You got it, Feia." He deftly tucked the Jeish into his Daush.

Smiling, Lafiel saluted. "Lyuf Raika, take care until we meet again."

"You too, Feia." Bowing, the old man slipped through the Yadobel; its whooshing noise signaled his departure.

After making sure everything was in order, Lafiel hailed the control room. "Requesting permission to detach and exit the Lyumusko."

"Authorized."

Lafiel put the Gooheik back on and initiated the detachment procedure.

"I think we've overstayed our welcome, Lafiel," Jinto commented as he slipped into the copilot's seat.

"Indeed," she replied. And with that, the Pelia detached, turned its tail on Sord Febdak, and began to accelerate.

"Oh!" Lafiel started.

"What?" Jinto panicked. "What's wrong?"

Lafiel tugged at her yellow, silky Daush. "I really meant to return it."

"Want to go back?"

Lafiel convulsed. "Are you kidding?"

"I guess you'll just have to wear it," Jinto said dramatically. A moment passed.

"What was that whole hand-grabbing thing you did with Lyuf Raika? Is that a perverted sex thing?"

"Ha! No, that's a common greeting on my homeworld. I was surprised that Lonyu Lyuf Raika knew about it, too. But now that I think about it, he said he was from the Earth age. It must be common to other Nahen as well."

Something didn't sit right with Lafiel. After a moment, she recalled her first meeting with Jinto. "I thought the traditional greeting from your homeworld was to jump backward."

"I've never heard of anything like that."

"That's not what you said when we first met."

"Oh yeah?" Jinto thought about why he might have said that, and remembered how he thought Lafiel was going to hit him. He had to play it cool. "Oh, yeah."

"So, you *lied*, then?"

"Lie is really such a heavy word."

"I don't like lies, Jinto."

"That's strange," he jumped in. "Neither do I! So, we totally have that in common. I mean—"

"Why did you really jump backward?"

"Well, you see . . ." Jinto mumbled feebly.

Under Lafiel's boring gaze, Jinto began to sweat profusely. "Well," she surmised, "it looks like we've found something to talk about on the trip to Sufagnaum."

"Oh boy," Jinto squeaked.

5 Safugnoff Sord (Sord Sufagnaum)

Jinto devoured a battlefield meal (Waniil), which was an entire meal condensed into a convenient cylinder of hypernutritious blandness. For some reason, the Abh preferred this to regular food.

It kind of made Jinto want to barf.

I wonder why none of the other Sash ever mentioned it. Maybe I just have dull taste buds. I wish I'd snagged some of Lyuf Raika's food for the road. Oh well.

"Jinto, we're within identification range of Sord Sufagnaum," Lafiel announced.

"Sweet." Jinto abandoned what was left of his meal and its wrapper, intending to dispose of both later, knowing the garbage would be floating where he left it when he returned.

"What's the situation?" Jinto inquired.

"I still can't tell," Lafiel admitted, staring at her screen. "There's a bunch of Flasath out there, but I don't know if they're enemies or allies."

"What do we do if they're bad guys?" Jinto looked at the screen, counting the space-time bubbles.

"We'll break through. We don't have the gas to go back now. Right?"

"Why do you even ask? You're in charge, here."

"So I hear. We'll pass into Sord Sufagnaum in approximately seven hours."

"I hope those Flasath are the welcoming committee," joked Jinto.

"The welcome could be much warmer than we'd prefer, if you catch my drift."

"Man, you really know—"

"How to brighten your day?" Lafiel finished his sentence.

"Exactly." Jinto batted at the remains of his Waniil, sending it toward the garbage chute. It missed the target completely, forcing him to unbuckle his seat belt (Apyuf) to retrieve it.

Two hours later, the situation became clear.

More than twenty Flasath loitered near the warped spiral of Sord Sufagnaum. Nervously, Lafiel tapped her finger on the display screen's map of Plane Space (Ja Fe).

"What?"

"Jinto, it looks grim."

"You don't have to say anything else." After a moment, he cracked. "Okay, I can't stand it. Fill me in."

"The Flasath aren't in a Labule formation—Star Force formations are always much more elegant. Sadly, I highly doubt these are Isath."

"I see." Jinto was still engaged in the futile exercise of trying to wrap his head around the idea of an "elegant formation." *Maybe they'll teach me at Kenru Sazoir,* he hoped, thinking of his future in Administration School.

Jinto sighed. "I guess we're going to be even more delayed in getting to Lakfakalle, huh?"

One of the Flasath started moving, slowly approaching the Pelia. Jinto's thoughts wandered to the conditions of the United Mankind's concentration camps.

"That's a very large mass," Lafiel said calmly.

"So it shouldn't be hard to outrun it, right?" Jinto hoped.

"True."

"Oh, good." Jinto couldn't imagine how it would improve their situation to evade one of the twenty potentially-hostile Flasath.

"Judging by its mass, I'd wager that's an Alek," Lafiel stated.

"Okay. And that means . . ." He looked to Lafiel to finish the sentence.

Out of the corner of her eye, Lafiel shot Jinto a glare, jogging his memory.

Battle-line ships were always equipped with plenty of mines (Hoksath). True, Alek were no match for Resii in a normal space battle (Dadjocs), but they were probably the strongest crafts in Plane Space (Fath).

On the screen, a blue dot represented the Pelia and a yellow dot marked the unidentified Flasath. Ever so slowly, the yellow dot crept toward the blue. After about an hour, the yellow blip stood obstinately between the blue dot and Sord Sufagnaum.

Lafiel pressed her finger to her tiara. "I'm getting signal. A 'friend-or-foe' inquiry."

"Frybar?" Jinto asked optimistically.

"No."

"Don't sugar coat it; I can take it," Jinto laughed through immense panic. "Can we fool them? Pretend to be on their side?"

"I would never be so cowardly!"

"Huh. I would. Maybe it's genetic," he commented.

"It wouldn't work anyway. Ah, here it is," Lafiel grimaced.

"What?" Jinto asked out of habitual curiosity, instantly wishing he hadn't.

"They say they'll shoot if we don't commence Skobrotaf."

"They want us to stop? Are you going to do it?"

"Do you want me to?"

"Of course not," Jinto lied. "I was just checking."

The yellow dot suddenly birthed three baby dots that moved extremely quickly. They were fast—even faster than the Pelia.

Steadfast, the Pelia held its course.

Is that it? Jinto looked for an answer in Lafiel's unwavering profile. *Has she given up?*

Lafiel kept her eyes trained on the Ja Fe display. A smattering of green- and red-dotted lines appeared. As if on cue, Lafiel made a movement with her Gooheik arm. Immediately, the Pelia lurched sideways.

Jinto watched the display screen; as soon as the blue dot changed directions, the yellow pests behind it followed suit.

Do they have to follow us? Jinto ground his teeth. Only the sight of Lafiel forging bravely onward kept Jinto from falling apart completely.

Who is she fooling? He thought. *Those Hoksath will follow us forever.*

Suddenly, Jinto understood Lafiel's strategy; she knew they could not escape the mines, but they could potentially run long enough to eat up most of the Hoksath's fuel. *She wants to reduce the size of their explosions!*

While dodging mines, Lafiel had to keep the ship moving toward the haven of Sord Sufagnaum. If they remained in Plane Space, the Alek would continue peppering them with mines.

If there is a god answering prayers somewhere, I've got a big one for you. Jinto wondered if he should have gone to church more regularly as he watched the lethal yellow dots zip along the display screen.

The battleship fired three new Hoksath.

"Who are these barbarians?!" Jinto shouted.

"That's a good sign," Lafiel pointed out optimistically.

"That they're blasting us with more bombs?"

"They wouldn't fire new mines if the first ones weren't nearly out of fuel." During this explanation, the three yellow dots closest to the Pelia blipped off the screen.

"Hey! You did it!" cheered Jinto. A beep from the Ja Fe reminded him that there were three more mines on their way to blast them to pieces.

"It's okay," assured Lafiel. "We can get away."

Sord Sufagnaum got closer by the second.

Manipulating the Gooheik, Lafiel brought the ship's engines (Sei) to life, causing the whole ship to rattle.

Because Jinto didn't have Frokaj, Lafiel showed the external scenery on the display screen. Right now, all they could see was the ashy-gray inner surface of their Flasath.

Behind them, there was an incredible flash of bright white light, in which specks of color swirled and danced about. The pieces of colored light grew.

So that's what Gor Putarloth looks like, Jinto thought, identifying the visual indicators of space-time fusion. *It's disgustingly beautiful.*

"Entering battle acceleration," warned Lafiel. Their seats transformed into reclining shapes.

Flasath were independent little universes that moved through Fath like rolling balls. However, the ship inside the ball remained inert. Thus, for the Pelia to accelerate, its Flasath had to roll. The colorful beam of light went around and around with the Flasath's exterior at such great speeds that it just appeared to be a continuous rainbow ring. Breathtaking, really.

And maybe a tiny bit nauseating, Jinto decided.

The Pelia's steady acceleration increased its gravitational pull on Jinto, too. They were inching upward of six Daemon already. Uncomfortable, Jinto huffed, "Think they'll chase us into normal space?"

"In Dath, we'll have greater agility."

"Well, I feel slightly better," he wheezed, as the yellow dots appeared ready to swallow the blue at any second.

Abruptly, the gray of the Flasath and the ring of color disappeared from view, leaving only pitch black sprinkled with faintly twinkling stars.

They turned around. The Dath side of Sord Sufagnaum looked like a huge, glow-in-the-dark ball.

"We're out! What about the Hoksath?"

Closing her eyes, Lafiel searched for the mines with her Frokaj. "Still coming."

Exiting Fath through a Sord was like playing the lottery; regardless where you went through the gate on the Fath side, you could pop out anywhere on the Dath side. It boggled mathematical minds.

Unfortunately for the mines, they exited Plane Space on almost the exact opposite side of the sphere, meaning they had to completely change directions to chase the Pelia. As they did so, they began to lose a lot of steam.

"We did it!" Jinto celebrated, but didn't let himself get too excited. "Are there more enemies?"

"No. At least, not at the moment."

"I guess they're more worried about securing the gate."

"Yes. They are occupied elsewhere. Look." Lafiel pointed with her non-Gooheik arm.

In the distance, Jinto saw a blue sphere—a planet. It was Clasbul, the only inhabited planet in Marquis Safugnoff's territory (Loebehynu Sufagnaum). On the dark side of the planet, lights flickered on and off.

"Right now, the enemies are all on the other side of the gate, trying to keep Labule forces from getting to Sufagnaum, where all the real action is."

"You mean there's a war on that planet?"

Lafiel nodded.

"Am I crazy, or are we still heading toward it?"

"Yes."

"Yes, I'm crazy, or yes, we're going there?"

"We're going there," she said.

"But there's a battle! A battle!"

"Where else could we go?"

Jinto blinked. "Good point."

There was no guarantee that the Labule would win a land battle, so waiting for it to end was not a great idea. Besides, the mines were still feebly trailing them. And there was still the possibility that an enemy might emerge from the Sord at any moment.

Even so, Jinto didn't like the idea of flying into an ongoing war. And he *really* disliked the fact that it was their only option.

"Rue Labule, please come in. This is the Resii *Gosroth's* Pelia." Lafiel called into her comms device.

"Roger, Pelia. To maintain military secrets, do not transmit any more details."

"Roger, Lonid Sufagnaum. Awaiting orders."

"Unfortunately, we cannot take your ship at this base. Proceed as you deem fit."

Biting her lower lip, Lafiel answered, "Roger. We'll do our best. Sathoth!"

"Yes, keep the dream alive, Pelia." He sighed then tried to rally his spirits. "Well, Sathoth Frybareri!"

And the comms device beeped off.

"They expect to lose?" Jinto checked.

"Of course," growled an agitated Lafiel. "Each Aith only has a small number of troops. You think they can handle a full invasion with only one Lonid Drok?"

"Sorry. Stupid question."

"No." Lafiel softened. "I'm sorry, Jinto. I was supposed to deliver you safe and sound."

"It's not your fault," he said instantly, as if by rote. It was true anyway. "So, what's the enemy situation?"

"Three ships are coming this way, but right now, they're pretty far off."

Looking ahead, Jinto couldn't make out them out. *Worthless lander senses!* He could really only see the planet Clasbul, which loomed large, nearly filling his whole field of vision.

Something resembling a piece of dental floss flaked off the planet, glinting in Sufagnaum's sun.

"What was that?" Jinto asked.

"It looks like an Arnej."

"An orbital tower? Why is it detaching?" Jinto wondered, before realizing the obvious answer. "Oh."

"It's not even a military structure. Those cowards!" Lafiel was pissed.

As usual, Jinto felt more panic than outrage. "True, but what I want to know is . . . can you land this thing?"

"Land it?" Lafiel looked at Jinto.

"With no orbital tower," Jinto shuddered, "we'll have to touch down on the planet's surface."

"Oh yeah. We should be able to do it."

"Should? What do you mean, *should?*"

An avalanche of Baronh poured down the display screen. Reading, Lafiel smiled. "The ship thinks it's going to work out."

"Are you telling me you didn't consider this until right now?"

Lafiel blushed.

"Then why the hell were we in such a hurry?" Jinto asked. *Crap, my body feels heavy. How long are we going to keep accelerating?*

"I always thought we'd be a part of the battle," Lafiel answered.

"We're not even armed!"

"I never said it was a perfect plan, but I can improvise. We defeated the baron, remember? Right now, there are three ships coming for us. Do I look worried?"

"No, but that's because you're suicidal."

Lafiel averted her eyes. "In hindsight, it does seem a little rash. Perhaps I should have consulted you first."

"Should have consulted . . ." A fit of fury overpowered Jinto. "Onyu!"

Instinctually, Lafiel's eyes narrowed angrily. Shame quickly overtook her, though. "Because I'm sorry I brought you into a battle with almost no chance of winning, I won't take offense at the spiteful things you say."

"I'm not being spiteful!" Jinto sputtered. "I just wish you'd consider living a little longer, Lafiel. The Abh have really long lifespans, so why are you in such a hurry to die?"

"I'm not in a hurry to die."

"It sure seems like it. Didn't you say you only fight when it can't be helped? Was that a lie or what?"

"The fight's already started. The whole planet's a battlefield, Jinto. When a Bosnal enters a battlefield, she fights. End of story."

"Fine. If you want to fight, fight. But I'm not a military officer yet, so maybe you should just drop me off first."

"Fine! That's for the best, because you'd be worthless in battle anyway!" she yelled.

"Look who's talking. What kind of damage do you hope to cause with this puny little thing?"

They glared at each other for a moment.

Lafiel looked away first. "Sorry, Jinto."

"Today has been the best day of my life so far," Jinto cracked. "Feia Lartneir apologized to me. Twice!"

"Ha ha." She was not laughing. "You're right, though. It's futile to fight in a Pelia. I guess we're both useless."

"Not true," Jinto pointed out. "I told you before, you're useful to me, and I'm grateful for that. Honestly. I know I can't help now, but I'd like to live until the day when someone else has to rely on me. Ideally, you'll be there to see it."

"Yeah." Lafiel sighed. The anger that temporarily overtook Jinto had swallowed his fear, and now that the anger was gone, so was the fear. His heart, which moments earlier beat like a techno drum line, went back to normal.

Oh well, Jinto thought. *Whatever happens, happens.*

In true Abh style, Jinto pushed failure from his mind, picturing only survival. At least if death claimed them in the void of space, they would not suffer for long. Maybe, if they kept accelerating, Jinto would pass out and just wake up in heaven. What an odd experience that would be!

A beep signaled an incoming communication.

"Is that Lonid Drok?"

"No. It's an electromagnetic signal from an enemy spaceship up ahead."

"Are they close?"

"Relatively."

Jinto squinted hard enough to see something the size of a dust particle glinting in the blue sphere. Was that the enemy ship?

Lafiel accepted the incoming communication.

"Pan dongu zop koth ri ji. Neik go shek!" A seemingly endless flow of gibberish flowed out of the Luode.

"What is that?"

"It's the official language of the United Mankind. They're saying they'll shoot if we don't stop."

"You understand it?"

"Yes. I studied their language at the Kenru. You will too, when you get there."

"That sucks. I've just started to get the hang of Baronh, which is not easy."

"Don't worry. Theirs is a simple language," Lafiel said. "Which is probably why it has no charm."

"Maybe so." Jinto struggled to pick out syllables of the language he couldn't understand. He thought he heard the message repeat itself before Lafiel hung up the Luode.

"Oh man," whined Jinto. "I was really looking forward to hearing you speak their language."

"These clowns don't rate a reply."

Eventually, the enemy ships materialized in Jinto's range of vision. There were three ships in a triangular formation.

"Good news, Jinto."

"Whoa! It's been so long, I've almost forgotten what good news sounds like."

"The main battlefield is on the far side of the planet. For now, those three ships are the only enemies in our way."

"Excellent," Jinto said uncertainly. "But their reinforcements can't be far away, right?"

"Yes, but the likelihood of them leaving the fray to fight a Pelia is nonexistent."

"Then let's go hide on that planet until the battle dies down."

"We still have to evade these ships, first."

Ominously, the vessels crept closer. With a sudden lurch, Jinto and Lafiel were temporarily weightless. Then, the ship snapped sideways, indicating the beginning of

Lafiel's chaotic evasive maneuvers. Jinto thanked the stars he was seated this time.

A quick flash of light ripped through space to their right. Jinto knew that, unless he was hallucinating, it was enemy fire—either a Klanraj or an anti-proton beam.

Bucking and twisting, the ship continued to exert a large number of conflicting gravitational forces on Jinto. All he could do was brace himself and try to keep his Waniil down.

Seeing an opening, albeit a small one, in the middle of the three ships, Lafiel pushed the Pelia on faster. Flying right through the triangle of ships was too tight to be entirely comfortable, but it was over very quickly.

The gravity fluctuations calmed down, and Jinto turned around to see only the opponents' propulsion flames (Asort) in their wake.

"Did . . . did we make it?"

"Yes. Even if they turn around, they won't be able to catch us now."

"Huh. Nothing to it!" Jinto congratulated himself on his excellent performance.

"Little do you know," Lafiel said pointedly. "That Klanraj that skimmed by was just twenty Daj away."

"How bad would it be if that had hit us?"

"We'd be a smoldering lump of plasma right now."

"You paint a lovely picture," commented Jinto.

Picking up the comms device, Lafiel began to grunt in the language of the enemy. "Kuu rin map ath tang kip!"

"What'd you just say?"

Sheepishly, Lafiel blushed.

Impressed, Jinto smiled. "Awesome!"

"I'm going to initiate deceleration soon, so don't say I didn't warn you."

"How hard are we going to brake?"

"Very hard. We've got a good head of steam going."

"Be gentle," Jinto pleaded.

"I can make it nice and smooth, if you don't mind burning up in the atmosphere."

"Hmm. No thanks—I don't like getting all hot and sweaty."

"Then you'll have to endure it. Here we go."

Abruptly, Jinto's whole body pressed against the seat; his ribs felt like they were going to snap. All his blood seemed to be stuck in the middle of his body, and his eyeballs nearly popped out of their sockets. Straining to look to the side, he noticed that the usually unflappable pilot was sweating, too.

Without warning, the display screen disappeared. No more blue planet, no more starry sky—just the milky-white wall. At the same time, gravity eased its grip considerably.

"What just happened?"

"Nothing. I just cut the Pelia's body loose."

"Oh. No reason to panic. It's not like we just lost three-fourths of our spacecraft!"

"It would be irresponsible to enter the atmosphere with a tank full of Baish. We don't want to blow everyone up."

"You just ditched the body of the ship!"

"Pelias aren't built for landing, Jinto," Lafiel explained. "Landing is only an emergency escape."

"We can land without the body?"

"We couldn't really land with it," Lafiel pointed out. "Sorry, I'm a little nervous—this is my first landing."

"First?!"

"I told you, I've never been to a Nahen."

"But there must be some kind of training or something!"

"I practiced in simulators."

Jinto tried to push the thoughts of their impending doom out of his mind. "What's scarier to you: the landing or the land world?"

"They're both terrifying."

For once, Jinto understood exactly how Lafiel felt. He clammed up to avoid adding to Lafiel's anxiety.

The ship began to vibrate—the atmosphere's violent greeting to the Pelia's Shirsh Sediar. It was the first time Jinto was glad to be ignorant of what occurred outside the ship.

The shaking stopped and the seats began to transform back into an upright position.

The unique sensation of plummeting through the air came over Jinto, igniting twinges of homesickness; it was the same feeling he once had while descending to the surface from an orbital tower.

I think I was just as scared as I am right now, he thought, *so nervous I couldn't see straight. I wonder what kind of planet this is, anyway.*

"Oh, I almost forgot."

"What?"

"We don't know anything about this planet. Do we have any data?"

"Yeah. It should be there, in the Datykril's Bowazebuku."

"Good! Datykril," Jinto commanded, "please give data on Loebehynu Sufagnaum."

The screen came to life. Under the main heading of "Loebehynu Sufagnaum," there were several smaller headings, such as History, Geography, Industry, etc.

"Please choose a file or give further instructions," the computer said in a monotone. "The commands are: reference, add, copy—"

Plugging his Kreuno into the armrest, Jinto interrupted the machine. "Copy all data."

"Copying," flashed across the screen a couple times.

"Thanks, Datykril. I'm finished now." Jinto pulled the Kym out of the armrest and patted the computer wristband. *It's always better to be informed than not. I'm glad I thought of it. I wonder where we're going to land?*

He was about to ask, but a jarring *THUD* shook the question right out of his head, replacing it with a new one.

"Are we there?" he whispered.

"Yes. We've landed."

Actual, natural wind blew their hair forward. Jinto turned around. The Yadobel door was open. But the actual Yadobel was gone—in its place, tall vegetation swayed in the night breeze.

"Let's get out of here quickly," Lafiel said, unfastening her Apyuf, "before they spot us from the air."

"Right," Jinto stood.

"Open!" ordered Lafiel, and the seat collapsed backward.

"Hey, cool! A secret entrance to your underground lair!"

"Onyu."

Beneath the seat, there was a small storage space holding the Daush that Lafiel had borrowed from the baron. She pushed it to the side and pulled out two Klanyu.

"Take one."

Jinto warily accepted the firearm. "I wondered where you hid these."

"They weren't hidden. We don't have a lot of space in here, so I stashed them while you were napping."

"Thanks for making that distinction." Jinto placed the gun in his Kutaroev.

"Take this, too." She handed him a backpack.

The bag, which held Waniil, a few tools, and a smattering of first aid supplies, was labeled in tiny, Baronh letters: "Emergency Landing Supplies."

Suspiciously inspecting the Waniil for expiration dates, Jinto said, "I think they're at least from this decade." Zipping up the bag, he slung it over his shoulders. It wasn't as heavy as he'd thought it would be.

Lafiel picked up something that looked like a necklace (Flarf) and hung it on her neck.

"Jinto," she said gravely, holding up the necklace. "This Flarf has the *Gosroth's* logbook in it. If I don't make it, it's up to you to escape with this."

"Stop it. You're creeping me out," he joked. Then he saw that she was serious.

"I just wanted you to know," she said, tucking the Flarf under the collar of her Serlin. "Datykril," she ordered, "initiate self-destruction sequence."

"Self-destruction initiated," answered the computer.

"Is there anything else you need from the Datykril?" Lafiel asked Jinto.

He shook his head *no*.

"I see." Pained, Lafiel took a deep breath. "Goodbye, Datykril. As a security precaution, please destroy yourself."

For the first time Jinto could remember, two huge eyes appeared on the display screen. "Roger. In accordance with known secrecy measures, I will render myself totally useless. I wish you well."

The giant eyes slowly closed as the machine executed the command (and itself). Once the eyes were completely closed, they disappeared.

What a downer! Jinto lamented.

Lafiel crisply saluted the screen.

"Let's go," she said, moving to the door.

"Wait!" Jinto ran and grabbed the Daush she'd deliberately left under the seat.

"We might need money," he said, inspecting the robe and its bejeweled accessories. "We can probably hock this sash clip for some serious cash."

"Money?" Nonplussed, Lafiel tilted her head. "I have money, Jinto."

"Huh?"

"Look," she poked at her Kreuno. "I have five thousand Skarl my father, Feia Loran, gave me."

Jinto's eyes were like dinner plates. During his days on Delktou, Jinto lived like a king (he'd thought) on twenty Skarl a month. He could stretch five thousand Skarl to infinity.

However, on a planet occupied by the enemy, what good would Skarl be? On top of that, her money wasn't tangible, just data in a computer wristband.

Still dazed, Jinto understood; although she didn't act like it, she definitely was a princess—she'd obviously never actually paid for anything herself.

He recognized the confused look on her face. "I'll explain later," he said, tucking the sash's silver clip (Apezm) into the bag. "Let's go."

They went outside. Jinto took a look at the vessel that had delivered them. Four wing-like protrusions jutted from the top of the cockpit. Knowing that was all that had slowed their descent, Jinto marveled at Lafiel's skill.

He knew that the Pelia would be very conspicuous from the air. They had to get out of there as soon as possible.

"You want to run?" Lafiel suggested.

"If you're up to it."

"What's that supposed to mean?"

"You might get tired."

"I was worried you wouldn't be able to keep up."

"You know, Lafiel, I'm more accustomed to running on land," Jinto said before taking off.

"Wait! Look!"

Jinto stopped. "What?"

Staring at the sky, Lafiel said, "The stars appear to be twinkling."

Jinto looked up. There was not a cloud in the sky. Indeed, the stars twinkled, but nothing looked out of the ordinary to Jinto.

"At the Arosh, I should get to a doctor right away," Lafiel said. "Jinto, I don't want to be a burden to you. If I go blind, take the logbook and leave me, got it?"

For a moment, he just stared at her.

"I don't want to crash your pity party," Jinto butted in, "but there's nothing wrong with your eyes."

"Please don't lie to me."

"I'm not. It's just the light of the stars bouncing off the atmosphere. They always twinkle like that."

"Seriously?"

In the faint glow leaking from the Pelia's cockpit, she could see Jinto was not lying.

"You think I'm smart enough to come up with an explanation like that on the spot? On all Nahen, the stars appear to twinkle. Feel better?"

"Yes, thanks."

"I guess someone fell asleep during physics class."

"Shut up, Jinto."

"As you wish," he said as he began bolting across the field. "It's hard to talk while running anyway!"

Tearing through orderly fields of grain-like plants, Jinto figured they might be in the middle of a farm. He couldn't tell exactly what was growing there, just that it was tall enough to slap him on the head as he ran.

The ground was damp, but not soggy—perfect for running.

Moments after Jinto and Lafiel had started scrambling through the field, a large number of electrically-charged particles (doubtless from the raging battle in space) rained down on Planet Clasbul like giant, green-glowing snowflakes.

6 Marquis Safugnoff's Territory
(Loebehynu Sufagnaum)

Jinto gazed at his new surroundings from atop a hill. Actually, it wasn't a hill as much as it was an enormous rock—a pumice-like stone full of cavernous holes.

Fields stretched to the horizon on all four sides of Jinto's rocky perch; even with incredible developments in the field of hydroponics, landers still preferred to grow their food the old-fashioned way.

Rustled by the wind, the fields resembled a golden sea; the giant stone was a lonely island. It was such a peaceful scene. It sure didn't seem like there was a war going on.

Far to Jinto's right, there was another island, possibly a forest. He thought he saw something move. *Is that a planetary transport facility?* Jinto wondered.

It was evening. Jinto and Lafiel had spent a whole night running from their crash-landing site. When the dawn broke, they'd stopped to rest at the huge stone.

Exhausted, they'd crawled into one of the stone's larger holes—it was probably almost big enough to be considered a cave—and slept. They were so exhausted that they'd barely had time to stretch out before they were sound asleep.

The first to wake up, Jinto crept out of the cave to take a look around while there was still a little daylight left. He took this opportunity to check out some of his Kreuno's data on Borskor Sufagnaum.

Viscount Safugnoff's territory (Borskor Sufagnaum) originated in Imperial Year (Ruecoth) six hundred forty-eight, when Soswie Wef-Sailar Daglei—a veteran of the Yaktia War—first entered the system.

The star system had seven planets, only one of which was potentially inhabitable. Before anyone could live there, however, it required significant terraforming.

Daglei, who would become the first Viscount of Safugnoff (Borl Sufagnaum), named his planet Clasbul, after the intimidating Soswie family crest, *Snail with Silver Twig* (Jath Syroegna Le Clasbul). With all the hard work of naming behind him, Daglei began to renovate.

The first step was usually to scrape a bunch of money together, as the modification of an entire planet was far from cheap. Interstellar real estate was a hot market, though, and investors weren't hard to find.

However, the Soswie family was already involved in real estate development, and had amassed an enormous fortune that enabled Daglei to skip the first step.

The second step comprised the actual terrestrial modification. With so much money to be made in planetary reconstruction, there were plenty of engineering associations (Gareurl Faziar Deiwim) willing to do the work. Daglei contracted with one such group to remake his new home.

The first thing the Gareur did was to alter the orbit of an icy planet outside of the Safugnoff star system, causing it to collide with Clasbul. In doing so, they risked destroying both planets. Fortunately, their pre-collision calculations were correct, and the result was a tremendous amount of new water vapor on Clasbul. Vapor became rain, rivers were born, oceans appeared—the dusty planet took a bath.

Next, they planted algae-like microbes, which replicated themselves at an incredible rate, producing oxygen in epic quantities. The microbes had a short lifecycle, and once dead, they degraded into soil.

With viable dirt, the engineers introduced plants such as sand grass (Ronrev) and lava pines (Rodorumzesh), which grew quickly. The plants reproduced and increased the soil's ability to hold water. As generations of plants came and went, the soil became more and more fertile, able to accept needier flora.

The engineers stuck some fish in the seas and some worms and insects on the surface. Essentially, the Gareur simulated eons worth of evolution in about fifty years.

Usually, as soon as a planet was ready for habitation, the developer started recruiting citizens. However, in this case, that did not happen.

By the time the planet was finished, Disklei, the second Borl Sufagnaum, was in charge, and he was not keen on letting territorial citizens (Sos) run wild on his beautiful planet. He did not explain why.

There was speculation that it was a science experiment—that Disklei merely wanted to wait and see if intelligent life would evolve. However, that was just conjecture. It was entirely possible that Disklei just wanted his own private planet.

Either way, nobody settled in the newly renovated world until Etlei—the third Borl Sufagnaum—commenced colonization. He made arrangements with the territorial citizens' governments (Fapyut Semei Sos) of at least a dozen overpopulated nations.

January first of Clasbul's year zero coincided with November twenty-ninth, Ruecoth seven hundred twenty-nine.

For his role in establishing an inhabited planet in the Frybar, Etlei earned the title of Count (Dreu), which also made him a Voda. At that point, the star system's name changed to Dreuhynu Sufagnaum.

When, in settlement year ninety-three, the population topped one hundred million, the star system was promoted to Loebehynu.

At the point Jinto and Lafiel smashed into one of its fields, Clasbul had an approximate population of three hundred and eighty million. Its lands were divided into twenty-one provinces. The provinces each had a prime minister, and the chairman of the prime ministers' committee was known as the Territorial People's Representative (Seif Sos).

Jinto shut off the Kreuno's historical recap and scanned the airwaves for a local broadcast. Eventually, he found a station. A middle-aged woman's face appeared on the small screen, delivering a speech that was nearly incomprehensible to Jinto. Apparently, language data hadn't been included in the Pelia's limited Bowazebuku, so he couldn't use the interpretation function. As he listened, though, he noticed that the woman was just speaking in a terribly disjointed Baronh dialect.

Once he got used to the Clasbul accent (which included atrocities such as "Au" for "Abh"), Jinto could understand the speech to a certain degree. However, there were also words mixed in that were not Baronh, and Jinto could only guess their meaning.

"We must please organize. Human race control together. Reason: they liberate us. Separated, control belong to Au. Now, we need build our government. Belong to us."

Essentially, the woman wanted everyone to thank the United Mankind for liberating them from Abh rule.

Apparently, the war on Sufagnaum had not ended favorably for the Abh. Jinto accepted the news calmly; he was prepared for it. Now, they would have to wait for the Frybar to recapture the territory.

Sighing, Jinto looked for a different broadcast. Eventually, an urban scene appeared on the screen. It looked like a movie.

Jinto grinned. *Who shows a* movie *at a time like this? Is this some kind of joke?*

Just like planet Delktou, the Abh had developed this world. Its people were those who voluntarily accepted Abh governance in exchange for a new place to live. Unlike the conquest of Martine, the Abh didn't take this planet by force, so anti-Abh sentiment was probably pretty thin on Clasbul.

Maybe the movie was just an indication of apathy— who cared who ruled Clasbul as long as it didn't interfere with the movie of the week?

The movie was pretty boring, but the characters' clothes fascinated Jinto.

Abh clothes were not sex-specific. Both men and women wore bodysuits (Sorf). However, on this planet, it appeared that only men wore Sorf. The women were all clad in sleeved dresses and knee-high boots.

He shut off the movie, hoping to use his computer wristband to calculate their location. Jinto scanned for location-signal electromagnetic waves. After he picked up a few, he compared them to the map pulled from the Pelia's Datykril.

According to the machine's calculations, there was a city called Luna Vega relatively close by. Judging from his map, the lonely island far off to his right had to be the city.

Should we go to the city, Jinto pondered, *or is it better to hide out here?*

The backpacks held only nine meals. With some serious rationing, they could stretch those for a maximum of five bland days. After that, they would have to get food somewhere else.

True, they were in the middle of a wheat field. But even if they could figure out how to harvest it, they weren't equipped to cook it. At any rate, the idea of camping out for that long made Jinto shudder. Surely Lafiel would find it even more trying.

All things considered, they should go into the city.

The only problem was that Luna Vega looked a little bit small to truly conceal them. At least it might have transportation facilities leading to bigger cities.

As darkness fell, Jinto climbed down the steep rock hill, which crumbled and gave way beneath his feet. He practically rolled to the bottom. Picking himself up, he found himself with the barrel of a gun in his face.

"It's me, Lafiel!" pleaded Jinto, throwing his hands up.

"Where were you?" Lafiel put away the Klanyu.

"Just checking out the scenery," he offered meekly.

"I asked where you went, not what you were doing."

"I was up on top of the hill."

"Onyu! What if someone saw you?"

"Don't worry. There wasn't anybody up there."

"What if someone spotted you from the air?"

"Oh." The enemy fleet would most likely be scanning the surface from above. They might have even spotted him. "I don't think it would be a big deal; I'm not wearing a Daush, so they'd probably think I was a local."

"You can't count on the enemy to make a mistake like that."

"Okay. I'll try not to do anything stupid again."

"Right. Don't do anything unless you clear it with me."

"You were sound asleep. Good morning, by the way," he joked under the setting sun.

"Onyu," she muttered.

Someone's grumpy. Jinto shrugged. "You want to leave, just in case?" he suggested.

"I think we'll have to." Lafiel stood. "Besides, it's boring here."

They ate and prepared to depart. Laden with gear, they cast off from the rock island.

"Let's go to the city," suggested Jinto, after they'd been walking for a minute.

"The city?"

"Yeah. It'll be easier to hide there than in this field. We'll learn about a whole new culture, too. It'll be fun."

"Isn't it dangerous?"

"Probably," Jinto answered frankly. "But no more so than staying out here. I can't say what the best course of action is, but I do know that we can't get food here, right? I'd rather take my chances in the city than starve to death or die of boredom."

"True," Lafiel agreed, sounding somewhat distracted.

"Is something wrong, Lafiel? Are you still tired?"

"No, I'm not tired," she snapped. "Why do you ask?"

"Just asking." *There she is,* Jinto thought, *the Lafiel I know.* "If you are tired, and you need to stop, just let me know, okay?"

"I told you, I'm not tired."

"Okay."

Time passed. The sky got darker. Night was upon them.

"Jinto," Lafiel called, "go on ahead. I'll catch up in a minute."

"Why?" he turned around.

"No reason," Lafiel's sounded disgruntled.

"It's too dark. What if we get separated?"

"Then wait here for a minute."

"What's wrong?"

"Nothing."

Jinto grew concerned. Lafiel was certainly acting strange, and he certainly didn't want to leave her behind. He had to straighten her out. "Listen, Lafiel . . ."

The princess listened quietly as Jinto launched into a dissertation on the concept of teamwork, the importance of communicating clearly, not trying to solve everything independently, thinking of plans together, etc. That's what it meant to be a team. "And now that we're in danger, we have to try especially hard to come together, and ride this out."

"You're dumber than a carrot!" she shouted. "Just wait here for a minute, and keep your eyes pointed that way!"

As Lafiel stormed off, clearing a small path through the closely planted wheat, Jinto obeyed her instructions. Apparently, even Abh royalty answered when nature called.

Jinto took a seat among the wheat, laughing at his own stupidity.

Meanwhile . . . after analyzing surface imagery, the United Mankind Peace Preservation Force's data gathering spaceship, *DEV903*, discovered a Labule craft on the outskirts of Luna Vega City.

The Peace Preservation Force tried to determine where the ship came from, but the records were all a jumbled mess, especially after the United Mankind engaged the *Gosroth*. They would have to spend ages sifting through all the war records to discover the Pelia's origins.

For the time being, the Peace Preservation Force had too much on its plate. So, everyone assumed that the ship's crew and passengers had most likely escaped from the comms base or Garish. From this assumption, they decided there was a high probability that the small craft's passengers were alive.

They issued a report to the intelligence headquarters and the higher-ups stamped it with "Low Priority," estimating that the key members of the Marquis' family had died in battle or were captured, anyway.

On top of that, the Safugnoff's private soldiers, called Principality Guards (Leitfeklash Sufagnaum), maintained a feisty resistance from multiple locations on the planet's surface. Many high-profile figures from the local governments escaped to join their ranks, and the small, spread-out flames of insurrection had to be extinguished before they united in a conflagration of defiance.

No matter who had crashed that Pelia, it would be silly to spend time worrying about it while there were so many other important tasks at hand.

"Oops!" Jinto skidded to an abrupt stop, sending clods of dirt sailing off the face of a cliff that gave way to a valley. *That was close.*

"What is it?" called Lafiel.

"Dead end."

It was still dark, making it impossible to know how far they'd gone or to see where they were going. Jinto tried to use his Kreuno's illuminating function, but the wristband's light was weak, barely enabling him to see the ground beneath his feet.

Suddenly, an extremely bright light appeared, reaching all the way to the other side of the valley. Behind him, Lafiel stood with her laser pistol drawn, its muzzle glowing brightly.

"How did you do that?" Jinto asked, examining his own weapon.

"If you put the safety switch into its middle position, that puts the Klanyu on illumination mode."

"I wish you'd mentioned that before I almost died," grumbled Jinto.

She shrugged. "I forgot."

He let it go. It seemed like only a rare set of circumstances would necessitate using the gun as a light. Jinto set his gun to illumination mode and squeezed the trigger.

Under the newly created light, the valley was wider than Jinto originally expected. Luckily, it wasn't that deep—just five hundred Daj or so.

"Intense," Jinto put the gun back into his Kutaroev and began to inspect the face of the cliff, which was definitely too sheer to walk down, but not impossible to scale. They would have to be very careful not to fall.

Rummaging around in his backpack, Jinto asked whether it contained some kind of rope.

"We should have some Ryurdauwa in there."

"That'll work."

Reaching into the backpack, Lafiel immediately produced something that resembled a stick. "What are we going to do with it?" she asked.

"Rappel, of course. Hand it over."

She handed him the carbon crystal fiber spindle (Jotmsei Ryurdauwa). He looked it over. It was military-issue carbon crystal fiber that looked like a slightly fancier version of the Ryurdauwa used on Planet Delktou.

The carbon crystal fiber spooled from the center of the stick through an opening that coated it with a quick-drying, synthetic resin (Geinyu). The resin dried immediately, enabling a person to grip the fiber without it slicing through his hands. This particular spindle had multifunctional, remote-controlled hooks on each end.

Leave it to the Labule, Jinto thought, *to have top-of-the-line equipment.*

Jinto pulled the hook and secured it to the roots of a particularly large plant.

"I'll go first," explained Jinto, "to see if it holds."

Grasping the Jotmsei, he slowly stepped backward off the cliff. Letting the Ryurdauwa out a little at a time, he kicked his way down the rock face. Eventually, he made it to the bottom.

"Your turn, Lafiel." He let go of the spindle, which began to automatically reel itself back up the cliff, scraping the resin off the makeshift rope as it went.

"Okay, here I come!" Lafiel shouted.

A loud zipping noise accompanied her lightning-quick descent—she must have let all her line out at once.

Jinto ran to her. "Lafiel! Are you okay?"

"Of course I am," Lafiel lied, wincing with pain.

Jinto offered her his hand, which she declined. Using the remote control, Jinto released the hook at the top of the cliff. Then he recoiled the fiber, leaving a pile of used Geinyu at the base of the cliff. He drew his gun and lit it up.

"What are you doing?"

"Looking for a place to crash for the night," he joked. She was not amused. "Seriously, I think we should call it a day."

They spotted a cave and ventured in. The dwelling was remarkably long. Even with their Klanyu lit, they could not see exactly how far back it went. Searching for hidden dangers, Jinto journeyed into its depths. Satisfied, he returned, dropped his backpack, and took a seat. He brought up a map on his Kreuno; they were about fifty Wesdaj away from Luna Vega.

Hungry, they ate. Through hastily chewed bites, Jinto announced his plan. "I'm going to the city."

"Right now?"

"Yes."

"I'll go with you."

"What do you think will happen if you go into enemy territory in a Labule Serlin?" Jinto argued.

Lafiel sighed.

I can't believe she didn't think about that.

"I'll go alone," he concluded, "to pick up the stuff we'll need to blend in. It shouldn't take long."

Lafiel shot him an evil glare.

What could she possibly be mad about? It makes complete sense!

"Fine," she relented.

"Good." Chugging some water to help force the last bits of his Waniil down, Jinto stood to go.

"You're leaving already?"

"Yeah, the sooner the better."

From the backpack, Jinto extracted three battlefield meals and the bejeweled Apezm. He put both into his Sorf pocket (Mosk).

Jinto wavered on whether or not to wear the Kreuno. On one hand, he wanted to try to pass as a territorial citizen. On the other hand, it was a valuable tool—what if he needed to contact Lafiel? In the end, he took the computer wristband off and added it to the weird assortment of items in his Mosk.

"Aren't you taking the Klanyu?" Lafiel asked earnestly.

He shook his head. "I wouldn't win any shootouts anyway."

"Don't be such a pessimist."

"I'm not. I just don't want to take a Star Force gun and risk blowing my cover."

Strangely, as much as going into an unknown (and potentially hostile) city frightened Jinto, leaving Lafiel alone scared him even more. The Abh girl, who seemed damn near invincible in space, had little common sense when it came to Nahen matters.

Well, she'll probably be fine out here in the middle of nowhere, Jinto convinced himself, *as long as no one finds her.*

But they might come looking for us. Someone might see her. Jinto's thoughts gnawed at him. In Clasbul's current political climate, being an Abh was immensely dangerous for Lafiel. He was sure her training did not cover this.

Jinto was lucky enough to have a distinctly un-Abh-like appearance. As long as he didn't tell anyone, no one would know that he was an Abh noble (Sif). If someone saw Lafiel, however, with her blue hair and Frybar uniform, the jig would be up.

"Be careful when you go outside," Jinto warned. That said, he pulled the Jotmsei Ryurdauwa out of his backpack. He pulled a length of fiber out the spindle's secondary hole—so as not to coat it with Geinyu—and carefully stretched it horizontally across the entrance of the cave at about knee level.

"What are you doing?" inquired Lafiel.

"It's an alarm system. Look, this fiber is practically invisible, and without the Geinyu coating, it'll slice through just about anything. If someone comes running into the cave . . . aaagh! Cut down at the knees! Brilliant, right?"

Lafiel tilted her head. "What if it gets a friendly person by mistake?"

He hadn't thought of that. Try as he might, Jinto could not justify setting a trip wire that could potentially sever the legs of a completely innocent person. But, Lafiel's safety was paramount in his conscience.

"That's a chance we'll have to take."

Once Jinto was gone, Lafiel sat down and hugged her knees to her chest. She dialed up a local broadcast on her Kreuno.

Jinto's Baronh was imperfect, but the language spoken on Clasbul barely resembled it. There were only traces of Baronh, interspersed with chunks of gibberish.

Lafiel gave up trying to comprehend the broadcast. Staring absentmindedly outside, she thought about her current situation. The circumstances had certainly changed dramatically; ever since they'd landed, Jinto had really taken charge, which was no fun at all.

Although it was her mission to protect him and the logbook until they were on a Frybar spaceship (Menyu), Lafiel felt as if Jinto were now protecting *her*. More than anything else, she was bothered by the fact that he seemed to know what he was doing.

It was a hard pill for her to swallow.

But can I really trust him to get us through this? Lafiel wondered.

Rubbing her calves, Lafiel sighed. Although she acted strong around Jinto, she was tired and sore. She would rather acknowledge the family cat, Horia, as her gene sponsor (Larliin) than have her legs burn the way they did.

On Clasbul, the surface gravity seemed fairly typical of Nahen (about double Abh standard gravity). Although Lafiel had experienced acceleration with gravitational pull ten times as strong, she had done so while sprawled out on an anti-acceleration seat specially designed to support her back. She never had to *move around* in this kind of gravity before.

Although Abh bodies were designed to work in the extreme conditions of space, they were ill equipped for Nahen. As she thought about it, she realized she'd never really walked so far before, even in Abh standard gravity.

Mostly, the Abh never intended to set foot on land. Even in dire straits, they knew that the likelihood of being able to crash-land somewhere was very slim. They learned how to land a ship, but were trained to just stay put and wait for help.

Of course, in this situation, Lafiel couldn't hope for a swift rescue; she figured that minimum time before help came would be ten days. They should expect a rescue to take at least twice that long—if it was coming at all.

In that time, the food would run out, and the scope of the enemy army's search for insurgents would expand. Whether he was dependable or not, Jinto was Lafiel's only hope of making it out alive.

As she drifted off to sleep, Lafiel smiled, thinking of Jinto. *He's been oddly excited since landing, even though we're in more danger here than in Lyumusko Febdak.*

When Lafiel woke up and Jinto still wasn't back, she was frightened. As they'd fled the patrol ship *Gosroth*, Jinto joked that he would do his best to look after Lafiel if it ever came to that. Now, that was certainly the case.

A Lartnei of the Frybar who never depended on anyone now put her fate in the hands of a lander Sif, the only person in a hundred-light-year radius she could trust.

You're the only one within a hundred light years I can trust, Jinto imagined Lafiel saying. *You're our only hope.*

On the contrary, she was quite cold and unaffectionate toward him. Jinto could not tell why this bothered him so much. Making his way along the valley floor, he came to a bridge. A bridge meant that there was a road. Roads led to cities.

Invigorated, Jinto sought a way to get up to the bridge. Unfortunately, there were no stairs or pathways. Literally crawling up the steep slope on his hands and knees, the wind fell out of Jinto's sails.

Apparently, he'd overestimated his physical capabilities. In hindsight, he definitely should have rested before setting out. He was distracted while with Lafiel, but now that he was alone, the true extent of his exhaustion sank in.

True, he was raised on a land world, but he lived in a high-tech city with an efficient transportation system. He wasn't exactly an avid outdoorsman. His limited physical strength came entirely from his Minchiyu days on Delktou.

She could at least say thanks, he thought, *for what I'm doing here.*

For a fleeting instant, the idea of abandoning Lafiel crossed his mind. It would certainly be easier to navigate the metaphorical minefield of the city without her.

Jinto shuddered, appalled at the thought. Even though he'd never considered himself a particularly noble man, he was disgusted by his own mind as he digressed into that spiral of evil thought.

Maybe, he dogged himself, *I could even get a reward for ratting her out.*

He tried, and failed, to make an evil face. Even without a mirror, he knew he couldn't look truly malicious. *This Jinto Linn character isn't that bad of a guy. He's not a great hero, nor a cruel villain.*

No, he's more like a comet hurtling through space with no control over its own destination, blazing from its proximity to a fixed star, sometimes tugged by the gravitational fields of particularly malevolent planets.

Putting an end to his internal narration of events, Jinto stood. Just as he'd expected, there was a road. As a bonus, its surface glowed faintly.

One rotation of Planet Clasbul took 33.121 standard hours (the previous night, Jinto'd slept almost fifteen hours). Human biological clocks were trained to understand twenty-four hours as a day, so the inhabitants of Clasbul made their days twenty-four hours. Thus, a new calendar day started with nine hours remaining in the planetary day. A calendar day might begin in the middle of the night, or in broad daylight.

The discrepancy between time demarcations was inconvenient, but easier to handle than adjusting the human internal clock. Besides, it was beneficial to dissociate planetary rotation from the living day. That way, there was no need to establish arbitrary time zones, which brought about a number of advantages in the planet's information network.

It was dawn now, but according to Jinto's biological clock, it would soon be noon. He would probably arrive in Luna Vega City around one in the afternoon, Jinto Standard Time—a perfect time to hit the shops.

Good thing I hustled out here, Jinto applauded himself.

He tuned his Kreuno to a local station and stuck it back into his pocket. Listening while he walked, he tried to familiarize himself with the peculiar Clasbul speech.

As Jinto's frustration of trying to understand the words decreased, his frustration with their content increased; it was an enemy broadcast, explaining the logic behind their invasion of Loebehynu Sufagnaum.

According to the speaker, the Rue Labule had started this war, arbitrarily attacking an innocent United Mankind exploratory fleet. Allegedly, the Labule Wikreurl (of course they were talking about the *Gosroth*) went after the ships without provocation.

To retaliate against this tactless act and to safeguard its new Sord, the United Mankind had no choice but to occupy Loebehynu Sufagnaum.

"You have got to be kidding me," Jinto muttered.

He knew it was a lie; he was aboard the Resii *Gosroth* when it had encountered the United Mankind's fleet, which was way too large to be collecting data. If the United Mankind weren't looking for a fight, they wouldn't have sent so many high-speed Menyu.

Jinto suspected that no one would believe his story. He changed the frequency, hoping for something apolitical. Unfortunately, the enemy occupied all the airwaves. Try as he might, he couldn't find a movie. The United Mankind was tightening its grip, he surmised.

One station aired a lecture on democracy and freedom. Another replayed that middle-aged woman's speech thanking the United Mankind. It seemed as if every station was devoted to exposing the evils of the Frybar Gloer Gor Bari.

Jinto tried to imagine how the citizens were reacting to these broadcasts. If this were Martine, where great hostility toward the Abh remained, there was no doubt in his mind the people would rally in fanatical support of the new rulers—new *friends*, as the middle-aged woman said.

It was impossible to guess how Clasbulians would respond to the news. Jinto saw no reason why they would forfeit their loyalty to the Abh, but he also couldn't come up with a good reason why they wouldn't obey a new ruler.

Maybe they just don't care, Jinto hoped, knowing that no matter which side the people took, fanaticism would put him and Lafiel in danger.

Maybe it was wiser to hide out in the fields, but close enough to town for Jinto to make supply runs. That decision would be easier to make once he saw the condition of the city.

A number of floating cars (Uusia) zipped past Jinto, but he didn't see anybody else walking.

Finally, he reached the city.

Thrusting his hand into his mosk, Jinto silenced his computer wristband. He was confident that he could understand the odd language, but he doubted his ability to imitate it.

I'll pretend to be an immigrant, he decided. *After all, that worked for me on Delktou.*

Jinto entered the city, where he finally encountered other pedestrians. Despite his best efforts to slink unnoticed among them, Jinto attracted a lot of attention.

What, do I have boogers? Maybe there's something wrong with my clothes.

Based on what the citizens wore, Jinto was decidedly conspicuous. For starters, his garments' colors were all wrong. On Clasbul, they were big on mashing together odd combinations of primary colors (as opposed to the solid crimson of Jinto's garb). On top of that, Jinto was disgustingly filthy.

Oh crap. I wonder if there are police here. What am I saying? They have to have police. They can't arrest me for being dirty, can they?

Uneasy, Jinto approached the heart of the city. As quickly as possible, he wanted to unload the sash clip and do some shopping. It seemed pretty common for the people of Clasbul to dye their hair.

Peroxide blonds and artificial redheads were everywhere—he even spotted a few with garish green and blue domes. Lafiel's cool blue hair wouldn't be terribly out of place here.

The city wasn't very big. From afar, Jinto thought that the group of tall buildings was the city's center. Closer inspection revealed that the handful of skyscrapers was the whole thing. In contrast, Planet Delktou's cities were huge sprawling affairs, comprising innumerable smaller buildings.

Here, the structures were primarily cylindrical, lit gloriously by their own external lights, which resembled trees. Wide streets ran between the towers, each with plenty of Uusia parking.

Arcing footpaths led from the parking lots to the buildings. Lawns and playgrounds littered the unpaved area. Jinto knew it would be beautiful to see during daylight.

Searching for a pawnshop, Jinto strolled down the street. He encountered a group of men in khaki uniforms.

Unlike the locals who wore one-pieces, these men's clothes had separate tops and bottoms. Each man also appeared to be armed.

Enemy soldiers!

Instinctually, Jinto lowered his head in the most obvious attempt to hide. Fortunately, the soldiers paid him no attention, laughing and joking with each other as they passed.

Once the men were gone, Jinto noticed a sign that read something like: "High Goods. Body Decorate. To Add Goods. Decorate Room. Buy Sell." Jinto took this to mean that it sold high-quality clothes and accessories.

Peering into the window, Jinto saw earrings, necklaces, brooches, and so on—all kinds of jewelry for the wealthiest of Clasbul citizens.

Feeling very out of his element, Jinto went inside.

"Welcome." A stylish-looking man greeted Jinto. The man's yellow and green Sorf had a thin, black collar.

"Uh, hi." Jinto said nervously. "I have something to sell."

"Good, good." The man smiled. "You have it with you?"

Nodding, Jinto placed the Apezm on the counter.

"Ooh, very nice." Picking up the sash clip, the man compared it to the grubby face of the boy who brought it in. He laughed.

"Yes, it is." Jinto's heart beat faster than was healthy.

"How much do you want for it?" The man set it back on the counter.

"Um . . ." Not only was Jinto completely unaware of the Apezm's actual value, he was also taken aback by this system of negotiation; he planned to let the shopkeeper fix a price, then hold out for something higher, and meet somewhere in the middle.

"Well," Jinto began, looking around the shop, unsuccessfully seeking a price tag to use as a reference, "you see . . ."

Maybe I should just suggest the amount of money I want, not how much it's worth. I might embarrass myself, but that can't be helped. Maybe a hundred Skarl . . .

He quickly kyboshed that reasoning; he had no idea what one Skarl was worth in terms of this planet's money. He didn't even know what the currency was called! He kicked himself for not researching this on the Kreuno before entering the store. Of course, he couldn't pull it out now. Suddenly, Lafiel didn't seem so naïve after all.

"Well?" The shopkeeper probably had other things to do.

"Hmm," stalled Jinto, "how about enough money to last a moderately thrifty person half a year?"

"That's a new one."

"Sorry." Jinto reached for the clip. "I'll come back later." "Fifteen hundred Dyuuth." It certainly sounded like a bold offer. For all Jinto knew, though, that wasn't even as much as one Skarl.

"How much is that in Skarl?"

"Look, kid," the shopkeeper whispered, "I'm just a businessman, not a nosy person. But given the current circumstances, I don't think it's appropriate to worry about the Dyuuth-to-Skarl exchange rate."

"True." Though embarrassed, Jinto was grateful for the man's advice.

"For the record," the man began, "I live on about twenty Dyuuth a day."

"Thanks," Jinto did some mental math. "Can you do three thousand?"

"You won't find anyone else in town who will match my original offer."

Jinto understood the man wouldn't negotiate. He conceded. "I'll take it."

"Smart man." Sliding a stack of cash toward Jinto, the man instructed him to count it. There were fifteen bills, each worth one hundred Dyuuth.

"Looks good to me," said Jinto, shoving the wad of cash into his Mosk.

"I'm glad we could do business together," the man said with a bow.

"Strictly out of curiosity," Jinto began, "how much do you think you'll ask for it?"

"It's a good piece," he said, turning it over in his hands, "but we don't wear Daush here, so we have little use for Apezm. But, it is well crafted and from valuable materials. All things considered, I'll probably ask thirty thousand."

"That's a nice profit," Jinto said admiringly.

"Yes, thank you." The shopkeeper smiled from ear to ear.

Now that he had money, Jinto needed to find some new clothes for himself and Lafiel. At first, he'd only planned to buy clothes for her, but after seeing the people, Jinto knew he stuck out. Luckily, clothing shops were far more prevalent than accessory shops. He remembered seeing several on his way there.

Jinto headed back the way he came.

A clunky-looking ground car (Frelia) stood in front of the clothing shop. A few people in khaki uniforms milled around it.

"You there, citizen! Please stop," blared the car's loudspeaker.

Jinto tried to make himself as small as possible. His efforts were unnecessary, however, as the soldiers accosted a young woman.

"What are you doing?!" she yelled angrily. People stopped and stared, wondering what was going on.

"You, too! The man over there." The soldiers grabbed a middle-aged man.

"Nothing to worry about," assured the loudspeaker. "If you cooperate, there won't be any trouble. Just give the soldiers your names and addresses and show them your identification, please."

"What did I do?" demanded the fuming woman.

"Dyeing your hair blue will be considered an act of insubordination from now on." Indeed, both the woman and the middle-aged man had blue hair.

"It's just a color. What the matter with blue hair?" asked the man.

"Any free citizen should be ashamed to imitate the Abh."

"You've got to be kidding me."

"This is ridiculous!"

Dissenting voices came from all around. Clasbulians seemed like a pretty rowdy bunch.

"You have until ten tomorrow morning to change your hair color. If you don't, we will consider you enemies of the state."

As the Sos reluctantly gave the soldiers their names and addresses, Jinto started for the clothing store.

"If you know anyone who has dyed-blue hair, spread the word that he will have to change it back to a natural color. After ten tomorrow morning, we will not issue any more warnings; violators will be shorn."

"I'm back, Lafiel!" Jinto hollered into the cave.

No answer.

I wonder how long it's been, Jinto pondered, *since I had someone anxiously waiting at" home" for me. Then again, is she really waiting for me? I've only been gone about three hours.*

The entrance of the cave was as he left it; no trace of blood on his makeshift security system. Cautiously, he retracted the carbon crystal fiber into the spindle.

"Lafiel!"

Nothing. Jinto started to worry. He took his Kreuno out of his pocket, turned on its light, and entered the cave.

There she was—a softly snoring lump. Lafiel looked surprisingly juvenile in her sleep. Relieved, Jinto sighed.

"Hey, wake up." He shook her gently.

Popping up in one motion, Lafiel knocked Jinto over and grabbed her laser pistol.

"Whoa! It's just me!" protested Jinto.

"You scared me."

"Not my fault. I've been yelling for the last five minutes, but you were too busy snoring to notice. I think you would have slept through—"

"Hey," Lafiel interrupted, "what do you intend to do with those tasteless clothes?"

"What, this?" Jinto pulled at his new, multicolored Sorf; indigo blue, yellow-green, peach, brown, copper . . . the colors were an eyesore, but the shopkeeper had insisted it was a good look. "You'd better get used to it. It's what they wear here."

"Gross," Lafiel opined.

"We have to live with it for the time being," he said. Plopping down the duffel bag he'd bought in the city, Jinto extracted a can. "Oh, here's a present for you!"

"What's that?" asked a nervous Lafiel.

"Hair dye."

"Dye my hair?" Her eyes widened.

"Yeah. I hope black's okay."

"No!" she shouted, instinctively grabbing her hair.

"You don't like black?" Jinto did not understand her extreme reaction. "I suppose I could go back and pick up some red or yellow."

"I don't hate black. I *love* this." She waved a handful of her hair in front of Jinto, as if he'd never seen it before. "It's not too dark, but it's also not too light—"

"Yes, yes, it's very nice," agreed Jinto. "But in the city, they're arresting everyone with dyed-blue hair."

"This is my natural color."

"I'm not dumb enough to debate that, even if it weren't true!"

"Kuu rin map ath tang kip!"

"I don't know what that means, but it definitely sounds . . ." he searched for the appropriate word, "feisty."

"I really have to dye it?" Lafiel asked weakly.

"I don't get it," said an irritated Jinto. "You'll putz around with your genes all day, but can't stand something as temporary as hair dye! The Abh baffle me."

"How many times do I have to tell you?"

"I know, I know. *I'm* an Abh, too." Jinto heard it a million times already. "But at times like these, I sure don't feel like it. Feia Lartneir, we've got to do this."

"Hand it over." She grabbed the dye. "I'm not letting you touch my hair."

As she started to take the cap off without even reading the directions, Jinto pointed out that she ought to take off her control tiara first.

"Take off my Alpha?"

"Of course. The goal is to make you look like a lander. Have you ever seen a lander wearing one of those?" Jinto suddenly had a thought. "Hey, I noticed that the Abh hardly ever take off their Alpha. Is it considered shameful?"

"You are so weird," Lafiel said.

"So, it's not, then?"

"No, it's not. It's just annoying to take the Alpha off. Maybe I'll just stay inside."

"Good plan."

Jinto's pulse quickened. A spacial sense organ was like a hundred thousand fully-functional eyes. The easiest way for him to comprehend it was to liken it to a bug's eye.

Imagining a grotesque third eye on Lafiel's forehead gave Jinto the willies. However, the sight of Lafiel's pretty face, sans the device, eased his mind. The Frosh looked more like a jewel in the middle of her forehead; a diamond-shaped ornament with the sheen of a pearl (Laf), it looked somewhat ruby (Doh) colored in the cave's light. Fortunately, it was far too small to make out the individual eyes. Instead of an insect-like compound eye, it looked more like a decorative piece of machinery.

Far from unpleasant, the Frosh was exquisite.

"Hmm, it's rather conspicuous," Jinto appraised.

"What, you want me to take it off too?" Asked an incredulous Lafiel. "You know it's attached to my head, right?"

Jinto laughed. "What kind of monster do you think I am?" He pulled a hat out of his bag. "Try this on."

Putting the hat on her head, she pulled the brim all the way down to her eyebrows, concealing the Frosh. The big hat also shaded her face, slightly masking her too-perfect features. Unfortunately, her "Abriel ears" still poked out.

"Hmm. See if you can get those elf ears in there, too."

"Right." Lafiel tucked her ears into the hat, covering them with hair. "How's that?"

"Looks good." Jinto grinned.

"Is the hat good enough, or do I still have to dye my hair?" she asked desperately.

"You'll have to dye it," Jinto confirmed, "unless you want me to cut it off. That would probably look worse, but it's up to you."

Lafiel took a moment to envision Jinto cutting her hair. "Okay, it can't be helped. We'll dye it."

"It's not the end of the world. Millions of people do it every day. Maybe even billions. Be brave. Remember, you're still the same person who fought Lyuf Febdak without any weapons."

"Shut up, Jinto." Lafiel glowered. "I love this hair."

"It's not a permanent change. Just while we're here."

"I definitely couldn't do it forever," she admitted, letting her hair loose from the hat. She lovingly stroked her blue locks.

The whole scene made Jinto feel awfully guilty. "You and the blue hair will meet again, Lafiel."

Nodding gravely, she poured the dye over her head. A high quality dye, it sunk into the hair, but evaporated immediately off her skin and clothing. It took less than one minute for Lafiel to transform into a new girl with a head of fresh, black hair.

"It suits you."

"Don't flatter me," Lafiel insisted, although she was glad to hear it.

"The next step," Jinto instructed, holding out the duffel bag, "is a change of clothes. I'll wait outside."

"Okay." Lafiel gave the garments a disapproving frown. By Clasbul standards, the outfit was decidedly color-mild. "What a strange Daush. Oh well, it's better than I expected."

Jinto stood up. "Just give me a shout when you're ready."

"Wait," Lafiel called, still digging through the duffel bag. "Where's the Sorf? I only see shoes in here. Should I just wear this over my Serlin or what?"

Jinto steeled himself to deliver the bad news. "It's not a Daush," he said slowly. "You wear it instead of a Sorf."

"I wear this directly over my underwear?"

"Yes. That's what they do here. On my homeworld, women do the same thing. We call it a 'one-piece.' Not sure what you'd call it in Baronh."

"I don't care what it's called!" She stared at the dress warily. "Do I really have to wear it?"

Jinto nodded.

"You're evil."

"I'm not doing this because I like to torture you," Jinto assured her. "Well, not entirely."

As soon as Lafiel finished changing, Jinto decided to take a nap. Lafiel stood guard. After a couple hours' rest, Jinto woke, stretched, and yawned. He felt refreshed.

"Okay, let's get out of here," he called.

"Yes," Lafiel agreed from her position at the cave's entrance.

Before they left, they had to get rid of any signs that the Labule had been there. Digging into the valley floor, they buried the backpacks, Jinto's old Sorf, and Lafiel's Serlin.

"That, too." Jinto held out his hand expectantly.

"No!" Lafiel clutched her Alpha to her chest.

"The military will issue you another one later."

"I know, but this is the first one they ever gave me."

"Then you'll have to come dig it up later."

"It might be useful."

"How?"

"I don't know; it just might," she insisted.

"We can't take anything that gives away our social status."

"We're taking the guns and Kreuno!" she pointed out.

"True." Jinto's patience waned. He hid the tiara, his Kreuno, and his Klanyu in the duffel bag before filling in the hole. Lafiel concealed her pistol in her Kutaroev, which she wrapped around her thigh. Her Kreuno was safely hidden in her shoe.

Ready for anything, they departed.

According to their internal clocks, it was evening. The road was no longer lit, but that was irrelevant because the star Safugnoff still shone brightly in the sky.

It was hot. Jinto envied Lafiel, whose new hat shaded her face. He regretted not getting one for himself. But money was scarce, and the new clothes had already cost nearly two hundred Dyuuth. That left only thirteen hundred, which needed to last until help arrived.

I wonder if these people would employ undocumented immigrants? Considering the laser pistols, Jinto decided that in an extreme pinch they always had the option of becoming bank robbers.

He grinned. *The princess and the count's son, interstellar bank robbers. What a duo. Sounds like a cheesy movie.*

"What's so amusing?" asked Lafiel.

"Nothing," Jinto lied.

"Glad to see you're not too worried about this."

They walked for a moment. Then Jinto broke the silence. "You think we look like siblings?"

"No, of course not."

"Darn, I thought we could pass ourselves off as brother and sister."

"Why? Is that really necessary?"

"Well, we can't tell them the truth," Jinto said, not sure exactly what the truth was. *Princess and loyal knight? No, I'm definitely not a knight. Hapless refugees? Maybe. Bene Lodair and her cargo? I hope we're past that.*

"You are so weird. If we must lie, we should coordinate our story."

"Right. It's something we need to think about. On Delktou, the Vice Prevention Police come running when they see male and female minors living together."

"I'm not a child," she asserted, "though I can't say the same for you."

"Once I told the man who raised me that I wasn't a child." Jinto recalled the face of Teal Corinto. "He just smiled and said, 'Children always say that.'"

"At any rate," Lafiel interrupted Jinto's reminiscing, "this isn't Delktou."

"True, but we don't know what it's like here."

If early marriages were culturally acceptable, then there wouldn't be a problem—they could pretend to be a young, albeit slightly shabbily dressed, couple on their honeymoon.

"Do we really have to worry about it that much?"

"I just don't want to attract too much attention. Normally—"

Lafiel stopped walking. "Would you be better off without me, Jinto?"

"Well . . ." Setting the duffel bag on the ground, Jinto rubbed his head. After contemplating the best way to answer, he chose blunt honesty. "It would be easier for me to hide out if I were alone, because I'm a lander."

"Does that bother you that much to be an Abh?"

"I don't know. It's not always easy, but I don't hate it. It's just, well, you can take a lander out of a Nahen, but you can't take the Nahen out of a lander."

"I didn't know you thought of it like that." Lafiel bit her lip. "Then don't worry about me or the Frybar. If you want to abandon your Sune, then let's part ways here. I don't want to burden you."

"Are you kidding?"

"I'm serious. I'll be fine. I can take care of myself."

"No," Jinto said sternly. "Although it wouldn't kill me to abandon my court rank, I couldn't leave you here."

"Why not?"

"If that's what I had to do to survive, I wouldn't be able to live with myself anyway," he said angrily. "You wouldn't make it on your own; you're not used to Nahen, and even though I'm not particularly interworldly, I'm still better off here than you are. Now, if you think I'm holding you back, although I hope you don't, then you go ahead and leave *me* here."

An Uusia passed.

Lafiel stared at the ground. "Forgive me," she appealed earnestly, "for wounding your great pride."

Indignantly, Jinto *hrumph*ed. "I may not know if I'm an Abh or a lander, but I do know that pride is not exclusive to either. I won't leave you until we're both safe. Okay?"

It was only much later that Jinto realized the magnitude of Lafiel's compliment; in the eyes of the Abh, "great pride" was an excellent trait.

"Got it. I won't bring it up again," pledged Lafiel.

Finally able to regain his composure, Jinto nodded. "I needed your help before, and I might need it again. For now, at least pretend you need mine."

"I won't have to pretend."

Upon hearing those words, Jinto decided that being an Abh noble wasn't so bad, after all.

"Yo-ho-ho! You two there. Hot Liipi. Is quarrel man fight woman? Woman there good. Leave man. Man resemble Shurip. Come with us. Good do Piiku."

Jinto looked for the source of these cryptic catcalls. The floating car that had passed a moment earlier—a sporty convertible—idled on the side of the road. Three men inside were leaning out, shouting. They were all about the same age as Jinto, maybe a little older.

Jinto flipped a switch in his mind to try to understand their bastardized-language, but they spoke too rapidly, mixing in colloquial Clasbul words. He couldn't understand half of what they said. He could tell they were teasing him and propositioning Lafiel.

"What do they want?" Lafiel looked to Jinto.

"Nothing." Jinto picked up the duffel bag. "Come on, let's go."

"Woman there Morun! Man there hold back. Kipau!"

"Shiik Ripiripi. Good Piiku!"

"Good. Stop Morun Woan!"

The floating car and its incessantly jabbering occupants cruised alongside Jinto and Lafiel.

"Hey you, don't ignore us!" The sturdiest of the three men jumped out of the car, blocking the way.

"Hyuu, Morun!" The man held his hand out to Lafiel. "Come, have some fun with us."

"Leave her alone!" Jinto pushed the man's arm away.

"Hey!" The man shoved Jinto, sending him rolling backward off the road, down to the fields below.

"Crap!" Jinto exclaimed, pulling the Klanyu out of the duffel bag.

Doing a good impression of an angry bull, the man was already maniacally charging down the hill. For some reason, Jinto didn't find the shove nearly as infuriating as he did the man's attempt to touch Lafiel. Enraged, he squeezed the trigger, not caring if it killed the offender.

A beam emerged from the pistol, striking the man straight in the stomach. Unfortunately, it was merely an illumination beam.

Checking to determine the extent of his injury, the man stopped charging for a moment. Upon discovering that he was unharmed, he resumed his mad dash.

Flustered, Jinto rushed to toggle the safety switch from illumination (Asertaf) to shooting (Uultaf) mode. He couldn't do it fast enough, however. The man was nearly upon him. Jinto noticed he carried a monkey wrench in his hand, with the intention to clobber.

Right as the man was about to beat Jinto, he fell to the ground, clutching his thigh. "Ow!" he writhed.

Lafie got him!, Jinto thought.

Finally, Jinto managed to get the safety switch in the right spot. He left the ailing man in the dirt, and ran up the hill. When he got there, one of the two men held Lafiel down, and the other tentatively tried to take away her gun.

Lafiel resisted, kicking the man off her. The men were confused; they definitely hadn't expected such a pretty young woman to put up that kind of fight.

"Let her go!" yelled Jinto, firing a warning shot into the air. It didn't work like in the movies; the laser pistol was completely silent, so no one even noticed.

Jinto pointed the gun at the ground, and pulled the trigger. Immediately, the beam interacted with the pavement, causing a small explosion. That got their attention; the men froze.

"Put your hands in the air!" Jinto shouted in broken Clasbul Baronh.

Liberated, Lafiel took a position beside Jinto.

"Don't shoot them, Lafiel," he whispered.

"Of course," she easily agreed. "As long as they cooperate."

Sensing the seriousness of their situation, the men stood perfectly still with their hands up.

"Okay, you two," Jinto said. "Go get your friend. He's hurt."

Glaring at Jinto the whole time, the men made their way down the hill without a word of protest.

"You're adjusting well," Lafiel noticed, "to this world's language."

"It's a gift. It's a derivative of Baronh, anyway." Jinto yelled to the men, "If you try anything stupid, you're target practice!"

"Shakkunna!" cursed one of the men.

"Thank you," answered Jinto smugly.

"What did that mean?" Lafiel inquired.

"I've no clue. It's probably not appropriate for a lady's ears, anyway." He shrugged. "Hey! Let's take their car."

"Commandeer the car?"

"No," corrected Jinto, "steal it."

"We'd be criminals."

"Yes."

They were in a tricky spot. The three scoundrels had forced them to act rashly; it was not common for people to carry around Klanyu. It would be easier to keep going down the road to lawlessness than to try to explain why two law-abiding citizens were carrying such weapons.

Jinto hoped Lafiel would accept the idea.

"Sounds fun," she said unexpectedly. "So, this is a robbery? Like you'd see in the movies?" "I guess," he said. Lafiel's enthusiasm made him slightly uneasy.

The three men crested the hill and spilled onto the road. Grimacing, the wounded man leaned heavily on his friends' shoulders.

Before Jinto could get a word out, Lafiel began to speak in very refined Baronh: "We are transient burglars, who have absolutely no connection to the Abh or the Labule. We're taking your car, which is a normal activity for robbers."

The men listened, dumbfounded. Jinto slapped his forehead. Even if they didn't understand a single word Lafiel had said, they doubtless noticed that she spoke in traditional Baronh. Their cover was totally blown.

"If you have a Kreuno or any other communication device, get it out," Jinto commanded.

Looking at each other, the three men said nothing.

"If you prefer," suggested Lafiel cheerfully, "we could just kill you instead."

Although Jinto doubted the men understood Lafiel, they flinched at the word "kill" (Agaim). Unfastening the boxes affixed to their hips and shoulders, the men threw them to the ground.

"Nice bluff," Jinto whispered.

Lafiel's expression indicated she didn't understand what he'd meant by that.

Shaking his head, Jinto looked back at the men. *They don't know how lucky they are that I'm here.*

Jinto told one of the men to put all the comms devices in a pile. After the man complied, Jinto incinerated the pile with his Klanyu.

"Okay," Jinto peered into the driver's seat of the floating car. In theory, he understood how to operate it. In reality, he felt shaky about it, at best. "Who wants to show me how to drive this thing?"

"This man was the driver," Lafiel pointed to one of the non-injured men.

"Right. You, in the car." Jinto indicated the driver's seat. Lafiel climbed into the back seat and Jinto took the passenger's seat.

"You two . . ." Jinto indicated the men still on the pavement. "Take a hike. Now."

Grumbling, the men started walking down the road.

"Okay, make it go," he told the driver.

"Most ridiculous thing . . ." the man complained, but shut up when Lafiel poked her Klanyu against the back of his head. Jinto watched the driver for a few minutes, and asked a bunch of questions. It was quite simple and didn't seem to require any particularly special skills.

The flying car used a system of electromagnetic repulsion that kept it aloft. It would only float on designated roads; if they wanted to go off-road, they would have to lower the car's tires. It had a pretty sophisticated autopilot function that only required the driver to input his destination. However, its manual controls were fairly simple as well.

"Does it have a GPS device?"

"GPS?"

"Something that uses electromagnetic waves to tell you where you are," Jinto explained.

"No. Nothing like that."

"Well, what's this?" Jinto poked at something that looked like a comms device in between his seat and the driver's.

"That's the navigation device. It tells us car's location, but it doesn't use electromagnetic waves."

Jinto rolled his eyes. "Show me how it works."

Pushing a button or two, the man made a map appear on the screen. A large dot indicated their current position. Jinto fiddled with it; it was really easy to use.

"If there's no GPS, how does the traffic department keep tabs on you?"

"That's an invasion of privacy. We don't do that on this planet."

"I see." Jinto nodded. "What makes you think we're not from this planet?"

"I'm wrong?"

"The girl in the backseat doesn't like being called a liar."

"Oh right. I forgot. You're grandchildren of Shakkuuna planet's first-generation settlers."

"That's right. And that's what you'll tell all your friends, too. Okay, take us back."

The man turned the car around.

"Stop," ordered Jinto as they approached the other two goons, who were extremely shocked to see the car again.

"Hey fellas, you're going the wrong way," Jinto scolded.

"We go where we want," barked the wounded man.

"Save it for the justice department." Jinto nudged the driver out of the car.

As Jinto slid into the driver's seat, he had a revelation.

"Hey, you guys got any money?"

"Now don't get carried away," warned the wounded man.

"You want us to shoot you again?" Jinto made his best expression of cruel indifference.

"Shit."

The three men reluctantly forked over their money— more than a hundred Dyuuth in all. It was more than Jinto expected.

"Well, gentlemen, this is where we say goodbye." He started the car and Lafiel climbed into the passenger's seat.

"I hadn't even thought about taking their money," Lafiel said. "You're good at this—have you done it before?"

"Ha ha."

During Jinto's stay on Planet Delktou, he'd always envied older men who drove around in Frelia with girls in the passenger's seat. He'd always imagined himself in their position.

Now, his dream was realized. But instead of a ground car, he was in an Uulia; instead of any old girl, he was with one of the most beautiful females in the whole galaxy; on top of that, she seemed to be looking at him with a hint of admiration.

So why did he feel so glum?

Originally, the Abh homeworld was a city-ship called the *Abriel.* After numerous modifications, they put it into use as the Imperial Palace (Ruebei).

Although the enormous ship was once home for almost a million people, it now had a population of barely two hundred thousand. Even so, it was more similar to a city than an orbiting palace (Bei).

The Empire never allowed foreign ships to stop at star systems under its control, but there were seven designated trade ports (Bidaut Alsa) for interstellar exchange. To facilitate trade, the four primary space nations instituted a diplomat exchange program.

The foreigners who lived in the Imperial Palace were ambassadors with their families. Like cities all over the universe, the immigrants in the Imperial Palace seemed to gravitate toward one particular part of town where they lived and worked. Sanpul Sangalini, the United Mankind's top ambassador to the Frybar, was one such political migrant.

The Frybar granted special privileges to the diplomats, but scoffed at the importance of their work. Sangalini and the others rarely spoke to any Abh higher-ups. An audience with the Empress (Spunej) was extremely rare, and usually occurred only when the diplomats arrived or departed.

Now Sangalini and three other ambassadors had a second chance to meet her, in the Ruebei's audience hall (Wabes Bezorlot), which was always reserved for important ceremonies and national affairs. Consequently, Sangalini had never seen it before. Aptly named Larkspur Hall (Wabes Lizel), violet flowers grew all over the inside of the auditorium. Sangalini found it unsettling, but at least the Abh respected nature in their own weird way.

In the center of the hall there was a circular section of the floor that was paved with stones. The stones were set in polished, black marble. Inlaid silver depicted the Milky Way. There was a platform supported by pillars that were shaped like an eight-headed dragon (Gaftonosh). Although the chair on the platform looked very comfortable, it surely paled in comparison to the Jade Imperial throne (Skemsorl Roen).

A beautiful woman sat in the chair, her posture extremely upright. Her elaborate Alpha also resembled the Gaftonosh. Pointy ears partitioned the bright, blue hair that fell onto her light-red Daush. Her irises were a stunning mixture of red and brown, and the whites of her eyes seemed to have a slight amber (Ftiainyu) tinge. Her delicate, white hands peeked out of the sleeves of her Serlin, clutching the cane (Greu) she used to command the greatest military force in human history.

She was Frybar Gloer Gor Bari's Twenty-Seventh Spunej, Her Majesty Erumita Ramaj.

Still standing, the four ambassadors faced the empress.

"Erumita," Sangalini spoke up, "First and foremost, thank you for coming to this conference."

"Noted, Ambassador." Ramaj nodded. "My time is limited. I'm sure yours is, too."

"Definitely," Sangalini agreed. He didn't want to waste a lot of time engaging in pleasantries with the Abh, who didn't even understand the United Mankind anyway. "I'll get right to the point. This is a protest."

"Excuse me?" The Spunej meant no disrespect. "I heard your nation's fleet attacked one of our ships—in Frybar territory, too! We don't have all the details, but I thought you'd have an explanation, not a protest."

"It's a protest," Sangalini reiterated. "It is certainly true that our army launched an attack in the area known as Loebehynu Sufagnaum, but that was merely in retaliation."

"To what?" Ramaj asked, raising one eyebrow.

Suppressing his emotions, Sangalini explained. "When our nation first opened a Sord to investigate the area surrounding its Fath, one of your nation's battleships ruthlessly attacked. We managed to drive it away, but only after incurring serious losses.

"Thus, I must protest on behalf of the United Mankind. True, the area was close to your nation's territory, but everyone should be free to travel in Fath. Unprovoked assaults cannot be justified or tolerated!"

"On behalf of my nation, I join this man's protest," said a visibly angry Marimba Soo-Nee, the representative from the Republic of Greater Alcont.

"And so do I, on behalf of my government and people," announced Gwen Tauron of the Hania Federation. He couldn't speak Baronh, so he used a mechanical translator, making it impossible to gauge his sincerity.

Speaking in a thick accent, Janet McCally of the People's Sovereign Union of Planets spoke unyieldingly as well, joining her colleagues in protest. "We have been continually subjected to your nation's violence and strongly request an apology with proportionate compensation."

With bored eyes, Ramaj looked over the four people in front of her. Her gaze settled on Sangalini. "Why didn't you file this protest before your ships attacked?"

"A local commander authorized the retaliatory strike," explained the ambassador, fully aware it was a lie. "As you know, in remote regions, far from our central base of operations, communication takes an extremely long time. If the local commander had waited for a decision, we probably would have done as Erumita suggests."

"You're lying, Ambassador." Ramaj tilted her head slightly.

"You have no reason to make that accusation!" Sangalini shouted indignantly.

"In the proud history of the Labule, not one of our ships has attacked without proper justification."

"This must be the exception that proves the rule," proposed Gwen through the translation machine.

"Even in an isolated case," Ramaj calmly continued, "no one in the Labule would ever start a fight he couldn't actually win. I cannot believe there would be a commander that would make two egregious errors like that."

"Don't you think that's a little one-sided, Erumita?" posed McCally. "I propose the establishment of a joint-investigation committee with both Abh and United Mankind participants, as well as mediators from the three impartial nations."

" 'Impartial' nations? Please! You're all in cahoots!"

"We are neutral regarding this matter, Erumita," said Ambassador McCally.

Ramaj spoke directly to Sangalini. "Ambassador, I expected lies from you, and you've exceeded all expectations. Congratulations."

Sangalini was speechless. What was he supposed to do if the Spunej never had any intention of believing him? Apparently, everything he'd worked to attain as a diplomat was lost.

"Why do you insist it is a lie, Erumita?" inquired McCally. "At least grant an investigation before you make up your mind."

"If you all honestly believe this man, then I have nothing to say to you, except that you've been deceived. I pity you, but the Abh will not entertain bald-faced lies."

"Erumita, if you start a war with the United Mankind, according to the Nova Sicilia Treaty, the People's Sovereign Union of Planets is obligated to declare war on the Frybar," McCally announced without hesitation.

"Why, thank you, Ambassador," said the Spunej sarcastically. "And if it comes to that, I assume the Republic of Greater Alcont and the Hania Federation will do the same?"

Two heads nodded in reluctant unison.

"Very well; you've got yourselves a fight," said Ramaj indifferently. "Thank you all. I wish you safe travels as you return to your countries. Your diplomatic status will expire in twenty-four hours. It goes without saying that I'll stake my honor on getting you safely to an open port."

That's it? Sangalini marveled. *I'm the most experienced diplomat in the United Mankind, and she didn't even give me a chance to bargain. I wish we'd had a better story! I'll just have to accept the declaration of war and return to my country. Oh well. At least I don't have to beat around the bush anymore.*

"Erumita, I hope you'll reconsider," said Gwen's machine. "You're starting a war with half of human society."

"Perhaps you've forgotten, Ambassador," Ramaj smiled, "that the other half belongs to the Frybar."

"If it's a fight you want, so be it," spat McCally. "But know this: An unethical Empire will never win!"

"Ethics?" For the first time that day, Ramaj's face showed real interest. "Perhaps we don't have any principles, but rest assured, that will play no role in determining the victor."

"I fear for humanity, if it's to be ruled by an Empire without ideals."

"Looking back throughout history, ideals are only beneficial to individuals," reasoned the empress. "When nations act on moral principles, all of their constituents wind up miserable. There are plenty of subjects in the Empire who harbor strange beliefs, like the people of Dreuhynu Bisurel, who don't understand that they are under Empirical rule, worship their Seif Sos as a god, and believe that the Abh are merely figments of their imaginations. There's the Sos of Dreuhynu Gogam, who 'store their intellects' in Datykril with the pretense that it equates to eternal life! The Empire rules all of them equally, and protects them all equally. If we imposed our morals . . ."

"Sophistry! A future under Abh rule—under a people who alter their own genes—would be intolerable!"

"You exaggerate," declared Ramaj. "Like you, we dread evolution, but after our founders were born some two thousand years ago, the basic genetic structure of the Abh has gone unchanged."

"You fear evolution?"

"Genetic abnormalities are the impetus of evolution, right? When we attained the ability to establish our genes as we wished, we simply put a cap on our own evolution."

McCally started to say something, but wasn't sure what, so she stopped.

"But, Erumita," Sangalini began, "can a nation survive with no principles except the fear of evolution?"

"Evidence says yes; our Frybar has existed for nearly a thousand years," countered Ramaj coolly. "Your nations may need morals, or at least the illusion of them. Otherwise, your consciences wouldn't let you rule citizens nor battle other nations."

"What makes the Frybar so different?" Gwen wanted to know.

"Our lack of moral conviction," Ramaj deigned, "enables us to unify human society without forcing people to accept Abh beliefs."

"If you don't unify them by belief, how can you control them?"

"It's a secret you'd never understand," said Ramaj coyly. "Now, lady and gentlemen, please leave. Your lies piqued my interest for a short time, but I've recovered. Lastly, I must inform you that we will win this war, which will be humanity's last."

"Permanent peace?" McCally asked, furious. "It's a dream! Many have tried, and none have succeeded."

The empress smiled. Luckily for McCally, it wasn't the infamous "Abh Smile" and there was legitimate affection in her expression.

Immensely dignified, obviously aware that the future of humanity rested on her slight shoulders, the Empress said, "Many have tried, but none of them were Abh."

After the diplomats left, Ramaj called up an image of Fath and projected it in front of the dais.

Normal space and Plane Space were like cosmically conjoined twins that had a botched separation surgery. There were approximately thirty billion Sord; the Dath sides all existed in the Milky Way (Elukufa). However, these did not logically correspond to the Fath sides of the Sord.

In Dath, the Sord were in a ripple-like formation; a central cluster encased by numerous rings (Speish) that increased in size as they got farther from the middle. So, the gap between the central cluster and the first ring (Speish Kasna) was slightly smaller than the gap between the first and second ring (Speish Mata). Gaps and rings alternated, making up the basic structure of the Milky Way Sord Group (Sordlash Elukufar).

The number of gates in each ring was the same, so the Sord were farther apart in the outer rings than they were in the inner rings.

Most of the Sord that humanity used existed in the relatively crowded Central Territory (Sorl Bandak), which consisted of seven Speish. Many of these Sord led to central Fath locations, enabling explorers to exit Plane Space through different Sord and come out in completely different ripples of the Elukufa. In this way, people were able to venture farther and farther into the rings of the Milky Way.

Eventually, the Unexplored Territory (Sorl Geiraza) became a misnomer. Regardless, it was still the common name for everything from the eighth to the eleventh ring, where Sord were scattered far from each other.

The Frybar started out with eight kingdoms (Fek), each with its own King (Larth). Ramaj was considered the Queen of Kryv. Similar to landed Voda who didn't rule their nations, Larth was mostly a meaningless honorific. Territorial sovereigns (Fapyut) reported directly to the Spunej, not the kings.

Of the eight Fek, seven lay in Sorl Bandak. Only Sord Ilik led to the outer reaches, where Sord were harder to come by.

The Abh viewed their single-frontier Sord as an opportunity, using it to take control of the twelfth ring (Speish Lomata) and establish military bases to prevent others from using Speish Lomata's Sord. The final step in securing this ring was to take over a small human planet in the Hyde Star System, which existed right on the fringe of the twelfth ring.

Ilish Kingdom (Fek Ilik) was also known as "Arms of the Abh" (Bar Seida); due to its shape, the kingdom appeared to be hugging the Milky Way Sord Group.

At the outer edge of the twelfth ring there was an anomalistic cluster of Sord which, it was widely believed, led to an entirely different galaxy. As long as the Frybar had Fek Ilik, no other nations could access those gates, and so only the Frybar would be able to reach the other galaxy.

Of course, the other four nations hoped to find a Sord that would lead beyond the twelfth ring, but that was looking less and less probable.

So what if we're blocking the path beyond Speish Lomata?! That's no reason to go to war, thought Ramaj. Especially when there are still so many suitable planets for humans to use.

Loebehynu Sufagnaum was in Fek Ilik. Enemy occupation would be comparable to amputating the "arms" of the Abh Empire.

"Faramunshu, are you there?" Ramaj asked.

"Yes." A hologram of a man with braided, blue-grey hair appeared next to the Ja Fe. It was Imperial Field Marshal (Rue Spen) Faramunshu Wef-Lusam Laza, the Army's Commander-in-Chief (Waloth Ryuazon).

"Were you listening?"

"Yes, Erumita."

"Is there any truth to what they said?"

"Everything indicates their intention was always to sever the connection between Vorlash and Sufagnaum. They've doubtless been researching the area for years, now."

"And the Spaude Rirrag didn't notice?"

The man said nothing, just eyeballed the floor.

"Are we losing touch?" Ramaj demanded.

"Probably," Faramunshu admitted. "We really didn't think they'd be brazen enough to pull this kind of stunt. Their intelligence was kept very quiet. I'm not trying to make excuses, but the embassy failed to catch it too."

"Yes," Ramaj nodded, "Lately, the Geiku Skofarimeil only sends concerns about potentially large-scale military actions."

"Without a doubt, the nations are working together. For such a ragtag bunch, they're putting on a good show." Faramunshu sounded extremely lively. Everyday diplomacy was rather boring for his taste, but war was an unusual game. Its novelty excited him.

But Ramaj saw it differently. No matter what she said, she was responsible for the lives of all of her subjects. If she went to war, so did they. She definitely did not want the blood of the innocent on her hands.

"Well, what about our Menyu that got attacked?" Ramaj asked. "The *Gosroth*, correct?"

"It was definitely a Resii. We're more than ninety percent sure it was the *Gosroth*. The Sord they'd used still hasn't been identified, but it didn't matter, because the only Labule vessel in the area was the *Gosroth*. I presume it was."

"You talk too much," reprimanded Ramaj. "Get on with it."

"Sorry. Now, Feia Borl Paryun is a Bene Lodair on the *Gosroth*. Although it looks bleak, the ship's captain, Bomowas Lexshu, was a highly-decorated Lodairl, and it's possible she was able to get Her Majesty to safety."

Oh, Lafiel! lamented Ramaj. *I liked that girl. As far as sons go, Debeus was so-so. But as a father, he must be some kind of genius. I wish she'd lasted long enough to be a proper officer, not just a trainee.*

"This must be a very difficult time for Feia Lalt Kryuv," someone said, as his hologram formed in the room. "Must be awful to lose a Yofu and Fryum Neg at the same time."

"Larth Barker." Ramaj grimaced, recognizing the owner of the voice. "Funny, I don't remember summoning you."

"Forgive the rude intrusion, Erumita, but this is a very serious matter." Larth Barker's hologram bowed. His full title was Imperial Fleet Commander-in-Chief and Crown Prince Imperial Field Marshall Dusanyu, or Glaharerl Rue Byrer Kilugia Rue Spen Dusanyu in Baronh.

"If you've come to offer condolences, you should talk to Debeus."

"That will have to wait, Erumita. I have come to get my orders for the Imperial fleet."

"For now, just wait."

"Wait?" he echoed suspiciously.

"Faramunshu," Ramaj addressed the Waloth Ryuazon, urging him to explain.

"Feia Glaharerl," began Faramunshu, "we've established that although the enemy has invaded Loebehynu Sufagnaum, they're moving slower than we expected. Right now, there is only one logical explanation for their actions."

"It's a diversion?" asked Dusanyu. "That's a good interpretation, Lonyu."

"There's no other reason we could figure," he agreed. "They would be happy to go over all of our data with you at Ryuazornyu."

"That won't be necessary, Lonyu," interrupted the Kilugia. "Battle situation analysis is your specialty, not mine. So, what are they going to do next?"

"Most likely, their ultimate target is Lakfakalle," reported Faramunshu. "They are very ambitious, Feia."

"Hm. Take out the Arosh in one blow?" Dusanyu smirked. If the Imperial Capital fell, the Sord linking the Ga Fek would be lost; the Arosh was the heart that pumped blood to all Abh cities.

"We don't know where they're going to come from. They could conceivably mount an attack from anywhere within the seven kingdoms in the central territory."

"That is why, Larth Barker," Ramaj added, "we must take precaution before acting. I'm putting you in charge of the Arosh defense. Faramunshu, help Larth Barker organize the fleets, please. Ryuazornyu can figure out how large a force we'll need; I expect it will be the biggest in the history of the nation."

"Got it. Any further orders?" Faramunshu looked to the Skemsorl for direction.

"Just one: get a move on."

"Your wish is my command." Faramunshu's hologram dissipated into the air.

"Larth Barker, did you need something else?"

"No, I was just thinking about your words concerning the dread of evolution."

"How very like you, Feia Dusan, to waste my time with your philosophical debates in the middle of a crisis!"

"You know you enjoy it too, Erumita."

Ramaj cracked a smile. "Well, that goes without saying."

"I was thinking," the king said, "maybe it would be better for humankind if we lost this war."

"Oh, this is going to be good!" Ramaj humored him.

"Consider this, Erumita. If we win, human society will find itself at peace, metaphorically sleeping. There will be no more societal evolution, which also means no more fear of biological evolution. Without the fear of evolution, there's nothing left to unify mankind."

"True; but if we lose, mankind will be forever crippled by that fear. You heard the ambassadors: they'd rather put themselves at the mercy of evolution than adopt our means of genetic regulation. It doesn't make sense."

"Yes, their victory would absolutely ensure a chaotic future. Right now, the four nations are united. Without us as a common enemy, though, they will inevitably fight each other. In the end, their squabbles will be their ruin, putting man at the mercy of evolution."

"Is that what you *want* to happen?"

Dusanyu shrugged.

"Then why do you bring this up?"

"Sometimes, I just like to think about the big picture, and our role in it."

"Feia Dusan," Ramaj said gently, "you have to wait until you're on the Skemsorl Roen before you consider condemning mankind to chaos. As long as it's up to me, we will work for peace and you will do everything in your power to help."

"Of course." He bowed. "No matter what torture the future brings, I'd rather endure it than suffer a loss to the Four Nations."

"I'm glad to hear your impregnable pride isn't getting in the way of your concern for humanity."

"Yes," he acknowledged. "I have a score to settle."

Taken aback, Ramaj raised an eyebrow. "I didn't know you cared that much for Lafiel."

"It's not just her. There was another person on that ship connected to me."

"You mean Dreu Haider's son?" asked Ramaj, surprised again.

"Don't act so surprised," Dusanyu smiled. "Someone's got to look out for that kid, even if it's just one person in the whole Frybar. Besides, I consider my role in helping to establish that family a great accomplishment."

Eighteen hours later, the Frybar confirmed the reports of enemy occupation in Loebhynu Sufagnaum.

Now that they had a car, there was no need for Jinto and
Lafiel to bother stopping in Luna Vega City. Jinto punched
Guzornyu City into the autopilot system.

According to the latest date in the Uusia's navigation
machine, they were squarely in the middle of the Loh-Hau
Province. Guzornyu, the capital, was a large city with a
population of more than two million. It would be much
easier for Jinto and Lafiel to blend in there, and enemy
troops would probably be easier to avoid as well.

As they ripped down the road, the shape of the crops
in the fields changed. Eventually, they drove beyond the
agricultural lands, through a smattering of forests and
plains, breezing through towns smaller than Luna Vega.

Jinto started to daydream about life on the lam with
Lafiel. He wondered what would happen if they didn't hide
out in the city, if they just kept running.

No, no. Don't be an onyu.

Of course, those three ogres would report their car
stolen (unless they stole it themselves, in which case, the
authorities would already be looking for it). Pretty soon
they would have to ditch the car somewhere.

Jinto had the sudden, stomach-tightening realization that they were criminals—now they had to be on the lookout for local authorities as well as the enemy soldiers.

"What's the matter, Jinto?" asked Lafiel. She had one hand permanently affixed to the top of her head to keep her hat from flying off in the wind.

"Was I making a weird face or something?"

"Yeah, you look so serious all of a sudden. It's making me nervous."

"Sorry, I didn't know I was supposed to be amusing you." He looked away, not letting her see his sulky expression.

"All I know is that usually when I look at you, I forget I'm on a Nahen."

"So, you want me to be happier, then?"

"Do what you want; they're your feelings."

"Do you even think about the words coming out of your mouth?" Jinto asked her.

The map suggested that they were approaching Guzornyu. Apparently, the city was somewhere in the middle of the forest. Shortly after entering the wood, some kind of indicator in the car started beeping, and the Uusia began to lose speed.

"What's going on?" asked Lafiel.

Jinto shrugged.

Up ahead, another Uusia was stopped in the middle of the road. Actually, there was a whole bunch of them lined up—probably ten vehicles in all. Craning his neck, Jinto looked for the cause of the congestion.

Halfway hidden in the trees, there was a group of enemy soldiers and an intimidating, metal machine. Jinto assumed it was one of the enemy's land vehicles.

"Uh-oh," said Jinto.

Think, think! I wonder if they're looking for us.

Even if they were looking for the Bosnal Labule who eluded three of their warships, they wouldn't know what they looked like. Based on their current appearances, Jinto and Lafiel should be okay. But, if the soldiers found their Klanyu and Kreuno, that was a different story.

Are they looking for this car? It was unlikely that an occupying force would mount such a large-scale search just to help out the police. But if the criminals were potential Bosnal Labule . . .

Should we turn around? No, we might as well just write "Don't Look At Us" on our foreheads. I wonder if we could outrun that vehicle.

Onyu! If it were slower than an Uusia, they wouldn't use it to look for one.

Crap.

Jinto ran through their options. *Turn around and definitely get caught? Or keep going and probably get caught? All we can do is put on a good show and hope they don't discover us.*

"Lafiel," Jinto whispered, "don't talk to these men; they'll recognize your accent."

"Right, and our cover would be compromised," she assented, excited to play this role of a criminal.

"Exactly. I'm glad you understand."

"What's that supposed to mean? Do you think I'm stupid?"

"No, but if you hadn't spoken to those three apes, I wouldn't have to remind you of things like this."

"Yes, that was probably a mistake," admitted Lafiel meekly.

"Yeah," he agreed. "And the next time we're robbers, you might want to consider using a fake name. Don't you guys have crime in the Abh world?"

"Yes, but it's not so complicated."

As they talked, the line of cars advanced slowly, and Jinto and Lafiel neared the front of the line.

Noticing Lafiel was resting one hand on the laser pistol which was still tucked under her clothes, Jinto gestured at it. "Don't even think about it."

Expression souring, she nodded.

At last, two soldiers sidled up to the car. One was jaded and middle-aged, and the other was bright and young.

"What's the trouble today, gentlemen?" Jinto asked.

"Nothing to worry about, citizen," said the young solider into a machine that translated his words and spat it back out in Clasbul. "Just an information inspection. We're monitoring the flow of people into the city."

Flashing a big smile, Jinto said, "Sounds like a big job." He hoped that the translator machine didn't translate his accent as well. He didn't think that was possible.

"Wallet, please." The soldier held out his hand.

"Wallet?" Jinto repeated.

"Relax, we're not going to rob you." The young soldier laughed like it was the funniest joke in the world. "We just want to see your identification."

"Right." Jinto's heart moved up into his throat.

Apparently on Clasbul, the wallet was also where citizens kept their Jeish with personal statistics.

Of course, Jinto and Lafiel didn't have anything like that; their information was all in their Kreuno. If he handed those over to the men, it would accomplish the exact opposite of his original goal.

Actually, the Kreuno Jinto had belonged to Seelnay. But that didn't really change anything. Jinto didn't think he could convince them that he was actually a woman, and even if he could, it couldn't benefit him to be a Rue Lef in this situation, anyway.

"The thing about that is . . . You see . . . well, I seem to have left it at home." Jinto fibbed, wishing he could have come up with something better.

"You forgot your wallet? That's a new one. I thought everyone carried one all the time around here."

"I usually do. I definitely get nervous without my cash."

Looking at Lafiel, the soldier facetiously asked whether she also left her wallet at home.

Affirming the man's suspicion, Jinto tried to smile as if this happened every day.

The soldier shut off his translator and jabbered with the older guy. They kept looking and pointing at Jinto in a way that made him wholly uncomfortable. At last, the young soldier came over and asked for their names.

Names? I can't believe I didn't prepare any aliases.

"Ku Dorin." Jinto stole his best friend's name, hoping it wouldn't be too out of place on Clasbul.

"What about you, ma'am?"

Jinto spoke for her. "That's, um, Lena Clint."

"Did I ask you? Let her speak. Or is there something wrong with her?"

When Jinto told her not to do anything, he didn't mean that she had to sit there like a statue. She was the only person Jinto knew who could do nothing *suspiciously*.

Her unblinking profile was too mysterious, too full of dignity, too beautiful. Inhuman, even.

"Listen, this is kind of embarrassing." Jinto threw his hands up in a "you got me" gesture. "It's a doll."

"A doll?"

"Yes."

"It looks alive." The soldier raked his eyes over Lafiel.

"It was very expensive."

"It even looks like it's breathing."

"There's a mechanical respiration simulator."

"Why is the doll riding in your car?"

"Is this a traffic inspection or what?" Jinto countered.

"Sorry; I'm just interested in your planet's culture." He was genuinely wanted to know what these Clasbul freaks got up to in their spare time.

"Okay!" Jinto shouted. "I'm really, really vain. I finally got enough cash together to take a trip, but had no one to go with me. I thought I'd look like a big shot with a girl in the passenger seat."

"Oh. Sorry to pry." The soldier looked confused. "Don't worry about it, buddy. You're still young. You've got lots of time to chase the ladies."

"What do you know?!" Jinto was really on a roll.

"Yeah, I guess when I was your age," the soldier recalled, sighing, "I did all kinds of crazy stuff too."

"Can I go yet?" asked Jinto impatiently.

"Can I touch it? It looks so real." He reached out toward Lafiel.

"No! Don't touch her!"

"Her?" the soldier inquired suspiciously.

"Yes, her. She's mine. I don't like it when people touch her."

Shaking his head, the soldier sighed. "Doll-love, huh? You're one messed up kid. You could have at least picked a happier-looking doll. This one looks like a real ice queen."

The middle-aged soldier said something, causing the young guy to turn around. After a brief discussion, the younger guy turned around to face Jinto.

Shrugging, he said, "Go on through. Sorry we took so much of your time."

Although he felt like jumping out of the car to turn cartwheels, Jinto just said, "Thank you," and pulled away.

Even after they left the soldiers in the dust, Lafiel remained stiff, like a doll.

"You can stop now," he said. "Thanks for playing along. It's a good thing you picked up enough of the language to know what I was saying."

Lafiel glared at him out of the corner of her eye. "As always, you came up with the stupidest possible lie!"

"You're not mad, are you?" Jinto ventured.

"You've wounded my pride . . . Do I look angry to you? Or maybe just *cold?*"

"Hey, we got through, didn't we?" Jinto reminded her.

"The logical side of my brain applauds your resourcefulness. The emotional side is barely resisting the urge to rip your arms off and beat you over the head with them."

"Wow! Well, I'm glad you're not an emotional person," joked Jinto.

"You might not know this, but we Abriels have notorious tempers."

"Yes, your family probably has the most infamous temperment in the universe. It's nice to see you fit nicely into the stereotype."

"It's nothing to be ashamed of! I like who I am!"

"Self-love?" he clucked. "You're odd. Seek help."

"Watch it! Emotion is about to win out over reason!"

Jinto knew he had to change the subject, and fast. "I wonder what that inspection was all about, anyway. They didn't even try to search us."

"They're looking for Semei Sos."

He blinked. "I keep forgetting that you can speak their language."

"I overheard them. They said they were looking for important people from the enslaving government, and that had nothing to do with us since our hair wasn't dyed blue.

"Slave . . . ? But the territorial citizens aren't necessarily submissive to the Abh."

"I know that, and you know that. And the Sos here probably know that too. But the enemy doesn't get it."

"Ah! They are misinformed."

"I think the younger guy wanted to know more about you. It seemed like he wanted to leave his post and hear all about your troubles firsthand, but the older guy wouldn't let him."

Jinto shuddered. "Yeah, that was close."

"I was hoping I might get to see that," Lafiel said wickedly, "even if I had to pretend to be a doll all day."

Passing through the forest, the car emerged into an open space.

"Is this the town?" Lafiel inquired.

On the left there was an expansive meadow. To their right there was a huge, meandering wall shielding dozens of towers in the distance.

"No." Jinto indicated the high-rises ahead. "That's the town."

"Then what are those?" Lafiel pointed out a cluster of tree-like structures very similar to the ones in Luna Vega City.

"Maybe a monument?" offered Jinto.

"A monument to what?"

"Beats me." Jinto had no idea what this tiny planet would have to celebrate. "But it's probably none of our business."

"You're no fun," determined Lafiel.

"Well, where I'm from," Jinto justified, "we have a saying: 'curiosity killed the cat.' "

As soon as they passed the "monuments," they reached the edge of the town.

Although the fixed star was still high in the sky, it felt like midnight to Jinto and Lafiel. There were few people out and about, and it was easy to spot the soldiers.

Jinto switched the car into its manual-control mode and parked. "While we're here, let me do all the talking," he advised.

"If you want, I can pretend to be a doll again," Lafiel joked bitterly. "But then you'd have to carry me."

"Don't be ridiculous! I would never lay a hand on the Feia Lartneir's exalted person."

Ushering Lafiel out of the car, Jinto took one last look around, making sure they didn't leave any of their possessions behind. *Well, car, it's been fun. Farewell.*

Even though there was no one around, Jinto spoke quietly. "Since we're leaving the Uusia here, it might be wise to go to another city."

Lafiel whispered back, "How?"

"There's probably an inter-city mass transit network. Most planets have them."

"That's no good."

"Why not?"

"What if there's another inspection? They won't always buy the doll story."

"I hate to admit it, but you may be right."

If the enemy soldiers conducted a traffic stop for no specific reason, then of course there would be others. And even though Lafiel had changed her appearance drastically, as soon as her hat came off she was easy to identify. Their best bet was to stick around in the shadows of the city until the ruckus died down.

Jinto made up his mind. "Okay, let's find a place to stay."

This is the worst day in the history of time.

Criminal Investigations Inspector Entoryua Rei obliterated another cigarette in his already overflowing ashtray. Jamming the butt repeatedly against the metal made him feel slightly better—it almost mentally prepared him to meet with the superintendent of the Luna Vega City Police Department.

Come to think of it, there hasn't been a single good day since the takeover. I wish they'd kept us out of their space battle, he thought.

The new occupiers had the police conducting numerous inspections, which made traffic a mess. People were complaining, and other problems would surely arise. Anyone who used the roads had to allot extra time for their daily travel. Delayed deliveries meant stores were running out of certain supplies.

And the soldiers kept making their own arrests, picking up everyone with blue hair and shaving it off right then and there. One of Entoryua's own men had a bald head courtesy of the United Mankind.

Don't they know being bald went out of style at least three years ago? he thought.

The worst effect of the new regime was the lack of good broadcast programs. For reasons no one knew, they'd completely demolished the holographic broadcast schedule.

It frustrated Entoryua to no end that there were at least six episodes of his favorite detective show that might never air because every channel was now devoted to cheesy propaganda.

Equally frustrating was the fact that although the United Mankind army was responsible for all of the sudden inconveniences, the Clasbul police departments received all of the complaints. No one even knew how to contact the occupation army's headquarters!

Figures.

From his office window that overlooked the City Tree Structures, Luna Vega seemed very small even though it was actually a wide, sprawling city with a radius of three-thousand Wesdaj from its center. True, most of that was agricultural land, but the rural areas contained houses and small villages. Eighty percent of the population of Luna Vega lived outside of the urban area, so there was a lot of ground for the police to cover.

The new occupiers prohibited air travel, effectively preventing the police from patrolling the city limits. Regardless, they didn't have time, as they were too tied up conducting the occupiers' pointless inspections anyway. In general, there was very little hope of the police keeping an eye on the city.

Four criminals had already escaped because the invaders insisted on accompanying the police, causing them to arrive too late to the scene of the crime. Consequently, the criminal investigations department was swamped with files of barely-missed arrests, which were annoying and time-consuming cases. Inevitably, the arrest rate dropped.

Naturally, people blamed the police.

Complaints weren't usually part of the criminal investigation department's workload, but Entoryua was a popular figure in the community, so he tried to help when he could. Then that morning he'd received a summons from Police Superintendent Aizan.

I can't believe that bastard, Entoryua thought. *If he wanted to see me, he should have given me the customary three-day notice. I know we hate each other, but man . . .*

"Entoryua here!" he shouted while rapping on the superintendent's door, well aware that Aizan hated loud voices indoors.

The door opened. Confidently, Entoryua strode into the room.

Wearing a wide smile, the superintendent greeted him. "Ah, Entoryua."

Usually a summons to Aizan's office was an invitation to calamity. Entoryua viewed the man's current demeanor as the calm before the storm.

There was another man already in the office—a young military officer from the occupying army who looked and sounded a little too friendly. Entoryua disliked him right away.

"There he is! Inspector Entoryua, the pride of our criminal investigations department." Aizan beamed. "Entoryua, this is United Mankind Peace Preservation Force Military Police Captain Kyte."

"Pleased to meet you, Inspector," chirped Kyte, extending his hand.

Entoryua just stared at the outstretched hand.

"Oh, excuse me." Kyte smiled, then brought his hands together and bowed. "This is the greeting here, right?"

Entoryua barely resisted the urge to say, "Yes, good boy," while patting the man's head.

"Nice to meet you, Captain," grumbled Entoryua instead. He turned to Aizan. "So, what do you want?"

The inspector already had a pretty good idea what Aizan wanted before he ever came to the man's office. He was almost certain the superintendent intended to subcontract the criminal investigations department to the Peace Preservation Force to help them with their pointless tasks.

Any police superintendent with a shred of self-respect would scoff at the suggestion, but Aizan didn't have the spine to stand up to anybody, let alone an army that had already locked up most of the planet's government officials on nonexistent charges. Aizan knew as well as anyone that there was at least one empty cell in the Luna Vega prison.

Personally, Entoryua would *rather* be in a damp, filthy cell.

"Have a seat, Entoryua. You too, Captain."

They found their way onto the office's reception couches, which were arranged in a circle. The couches were really low to the ground, so Entoryua had to stick his legs way out in front of him.

"Would you care for some tea, Captain?" asked Aizan.

Smiling, Kyte nodded politely.

Without consulting Entoryua, Aizan announced an order for three cups of mint tea. And just like that, three cups of tea rose through a machine in the middle of the circle. More irritated than thirsty, Entoryua just watched as the other two men sipped their drinks.

"Can we get to the point already?" Entoryua demanded when he could no longer stand it. "I'm really busy these days!"

"There's no reason to get flustered, Inspector."

"He makes a good point," said Kyte. "This is a very pressing matter."

"Indeed," agreed Aizan. "Entoryua, the captain here has agreed to cooperate with us."

"What?" Entoryua wasn't quite sure what that meant. "The occupying army is going to cooperate with us?"

" 'Liberation' army," corrected Kyte.

"I think you need a new translation machine, pal. Or maybe I need a new dictionary, because the last time I checked—"

"We've come to liberate you from the oppression of those synthetic humans, the Abh. We're here to inform you about democracy."

"We know all about democracy. Even Superintendent Aizan won his position in a 'fair' election." In this example, Entoryua opined, democracy failed miserably.

"Yours is a slave democracy. It's all for show. Your leaders accept Abh rule unquestioningly. Good leaders direct a strike against an oppressive controlling machine."

"Are you talking about Chairman Kindy?" Entoryua clarified. "I'd say he's a good man, even though I'm a staunch Democrat, and he's a die-hard Liberal."

"Democratic party, Liberal party—the fact that political parties have such names on an Abh-governed planet is sacrilegious to democracy."

"That's no reason to put them all in jail."

"Jail? Hardly. It's democracy school," Kyte said logically.

"It sure seems like an internment camp to me."

"It's a school. An educational institution."

"Oho!" Entoryua snorted. "It's the first school I've ever heard of that only accepts people who don't apply!"

"There's no need to be rude, Entoryua," Aizan finally interceded.

Coward. Entoryua quietly judged Aizan.

"No, it's fine, Mister Aizan," Kyte said calmly. "This is a misunderstanding—one that we predicted, of course. It's our mission to clear up these misconceptions."

"For a young man, you've got a lot of character," Aizan praised.

Entoryua had a theory that there were two kinds of "good" people: passively good and actively good. The former were non-intrusive in their benevolence, but the latter tried to reshape the rest of the world in their image— they were militantly "good."

Captain Kyte was, Entoryua decided, an actively good person. Nothing could ever be good enough for this kind of person, except remodeling the entire universe to his own ideal standards. Kyte would find fault in absolutely everything and everyone and happily point it out.

"I thought you said this was urgent," Entoryua reminded them. "What kind of 'cooperation' are we talking about here? Will the captain be reporting to me, now?"

"Such rudeness!" rebuked Aizan.

"It is natural for the inspector to be suspicious. So I'll do my best to answer any questions he may have," the captain said.

"Thanks." Entoryua bit out.

"We'd like your help with a specific case. There was a carjacking yesterday in which a citizen from this city was injured. We are very concerned about this."

He can't be serious. They brought me here for a carjacking? There's got to be more to it than meets the eye.

"What's the case number?" Entoryua asked.

Aizan rattled off the number from memory. Plugging his comms device into the police data network, Entoryua brought up the report on his display screen.

"These are the victims?" Entoryua laughed; the three men were hardly strangers to the police department.

"What's so funny?" Kyte asked.

"These guys are notorious criminals; there's no way they stopped to help two hitchhikers. Let me translate this report. They said they 'stopped to help a man and a woman.' That really means they stopped to help themselves to the woman. Whatever happened to them, I'm positive they had it coming. If a single word of this is true, that'd surprise me more than your occupation of Clasbul."

"Liberation," corrected Kyte.

Ignoring him, Entoryua finished reading the document. "So, what's your interest in this case?"

"You'll notice, it says the female spoke Baronh and was beautiful like an Abh."

"I read that. But you can't rely on crooks to give you a straight story. They couldn't tell Abh speech from a warbling bird. And as far they're concerned, women are all either 'gorgeous' or 'dogs.' This report doesn't mean anything."

"The man with her probably isn't an Abh," Kyte carried on as if he hadn't heard the inspector. "They said he spoke the local language, albeit poorly, and that he looked much more common. My guess is that it was an Abh female and an Imperial citizen."

"Why would an Abh be on the ground? Entoryua could not be convinced. "That's the last thing they'd ever do! They go crazy on land."

"Now this is purely speculation, but I have a possible solution. There was a Labule landing shell a considerable distance from here. Our army is trying to see if the two incidents are connected."

"So, you think the hitchhikers are the two passengers from the landing shell?"

"There's a high probability of that, yes," the captain admitted. "As you said, the female may not be an Abh, but it's worth investigating. I will do everything I can to help you in this investigation, but I will exercise the right to extradite these criminals once they're caught."

"They've got to answer for some very serious crimes here on Clasbul first."

"It's already settled," Aizan said. "You have no say in this matter."

Entoryua scowled. "Okay, boss. Whatever you say."

"So it's fine?" Kyte checked.

"You heard the man. It's already settled." He took a moment to skim the document again. "Looks like Inspector Bakuunin's in charge of this one. I'll introduce you right away."

Both Aizan and Entoryua knew that Bakuunin and his cronies had only solved three cases in the last three years.

"Actually," Aizan spoke up, "I want you to take command of this one, Entoryua."

"Me?" Even though he saw it coming a mile away, Entoryua tried to escape the inevitable.

"Yes. Please cooperate with Captain Kyte. This is a top priority. I don't care how many men it takes, just catch the bastards!"

"It's too much, Superintendent. I already have an overflowing caseload."

"Police get reassigned all the time."

"Only for huge incidents."

"This is huge. It involves the occupation—I mean, liberation army."

The fact that Aizan corrected himself only added fuel to Entoryua's burning hatred of the man. Submitting immediately to outside influence, the superintendent would turn the whole police organization upside down. He never dealt with issues by degree of actual importance, but by which case would look best in the news.

If he would just let the organization make its own decisions, everything would be fine. But the superintendent was addicted to making budget cuts at Congress' request. And after slashing the resources, Aizan invariably increased the demands on the department. It made Entoryua furious.

"There's one thing I still don't get," Entoryua said to Kyte. "You're looking for an Abh person?"

"Don't forget the Rue Lef. Equally degenerate, he defected to the oppressive regime even though he was born free."

"No matter; there are enough of you that you shouldn't need help from a rural police force."

"Entoryua, the captain is helping *us*." Aizan justified.

"Cut the crap, Superintendent. Captain, how many men do you have?"

Kyte puffed out his chest proudly. "I am a commissioned officer who is allowed independent action."

"So . . . zero?" Turning to Aizan, Entoryua threw his hands up pleadingly.

"This is a great opportunity for you, Inspector," Kyte said passionately. "Because we know little about your world, it is our intention to build a partnership with the local police that will help us unmask the enslaved democrats. However, in this case, they will not be tried according to Clasbul law."

"It's our job to catch them," Entoryua reasoned, "but how is that a big opportunity?"

"It's a chance for you to serve true democracy." Kyte spoke reverently. "Just between us, the higher-ups have discussed dismantling your police organization because it is a violent organization of an enslaved democracy. However, if you help us, that demonstrates your willingness to be reborn as an organization of true democracy."

"Sounds great. Are you sure you're not alone in that opinion?"

"No. The idea of reshaping preexisting organizations is gaining support. Even the supreme commander thinks it's a good idea. He just needs proof that it can work."

"So you understand, Entoryua," Aizan concluded, "we have to demonstrate the police's raison d'etre with our actions."

Maybe you should justify your own "raison d'etre," thought Entoryua bitterly.

"Why don't you work with the captain yourself, Superintendent?" Entoryua proposed. When Aizan seriously began to consider it, Entoryua retracted the offer—he couldn't subject his men to a case under Aizan's command. "Never mind. I'll take the case."

Entoryua lit a cigarette.

Kyte coughed. "What's that?"

"You telling me you've never seen a cigarette?"

"That's a cigarette? They're legal here?"

"Would a policeman smoke one, if they weren't?"

"Those disgusting things have been banned in our society for more than two-hundred years now."

"Wow. Don't worry—this one's odorless. Besides, it helps calm me down."

"It's the medical effects, not the odor, that are a problem," Kyte said as if reciting a grade-school lesson. "Controlling your nerves with mild stimulants is illogical to say the least. This demonstrates the dreadfulness of your enslaved democracy. It will be the liberation army's responsibility to criminalize these drugs and deprogram people's reasons for seeking them out."

Furrowing his brow, Entoryua took a particularly long drag on his cigarette.

In that case, Mister Military Police Captain Kyte, I'm convinced—from now on, it's enslaved democracy or nothing.

"What a lovely morning," Jinto joked, watching the sun set.

"Feels like midday to me," said Lafiel from her position on the sofa, where she sat paying slightly more attention to a holo-broadcast than to Jinto.

"Have you picked up any of the language yet?" asked Jinto.

"A little."

The holo-broadcast receiver was a flat box, like a miniature stage for the images projected in three dimensions on its surface. Currently, it depicted a woman speaking flatly about "Abh tyranny."

"Another speech from the occupation army, huh? Is this one interesting?" Jinto asked.

"No. But there's nothing else to do."

Nodding, Jinto considered their possible options for recreation. Basically, all they could do was talk or watch holo-broadcasts. They didn't even have a deck of cards.

Unfortunately, Clasbul didn't have much to choose from in the way of holo-programming. Jinto reckoned that Clasbul probably had better shows under normal circumstances. However, now that the occupation army controlled the broadcast companies, propaganda speeches dominated the airwaves.

"Have you eaten anything?" asked Jinto.

"No, not yet."

"I was thinking about making some breakfast." He yawned and stretched. "While I'm at it, I'll make you some lunch. What do you want?"

"It doesn't matter. I probably won't like anything we've got." Lafiel wasn't trying to be rude, just honest—she was definitely not accustomed to Nahen food.

Smiling, Jinto rummaged through a bag in the corner and produced a can. "How about Bolkos-style red eggplant stew with beef and kidney beans?"

Jinto did not know where Bolkos was, nor how they prepared their stew, but it certainly sounded exciting. He pushed the can into the automatic cookstand's input cavity and set the taste-concentration dial to medium. As soon as he put his large bowl on the filling stand, the machine purred to life.

After Jinto and Lafiel had abandoned the car, they'd set out on foot to find a place to stay. A short search led them to the Limzeil Pavilion Inn. They were excited to find it and paid for ten days up front. They were now solidly invested in their third day.

Their suite had two large rooms—a living room and a bedroom—plus a small bathroom. There was no kitchen, but the automatic cookstand in the corner of the living room enabled them to prepare simple meals. The couch and holo-broadcast receiver were also in the living room.

After stocking up on food, neither Jinto nor Lafiel dared to venture out of the inn.

I wonder if they've noticed?

They'd signed the inn's register as Jinto Sai and Lena Sai, having prepared the story that they were siblings. No one had asked though, so they hadn't volunteered any info. Maybe early marriages were common on Clasbul and the concierge had just assumed they were newlyweds.

No matter what their relationship, it was strange for them to stay in their room for three days. On Delktou, where everyone took great interest in the affairs of strangers, people would most certainly investigate the unusual behavior.

But what were Clasbul people like? Would the receptionist think twice about their young age? Or was failure to pay the room fee the only thing that would attract her attention?

Jinto imagined days passing and the receptionist at the front desk gabbing with friends. "*I don't know what they're doing in there. Three, four, five days. Not a peep.*" He hoped that wouldn't happen.

Jinto sighed. Maybe it would be a good idea for him to go out from time to time, if for no other reason than to alleviate his newfound sense of imprisonment.

They slept in shifts for three reasons. The first was that there was only one bed. The second was that they thought it was a good idea for one person to keep watch. The third and most important reason was that they knew they couldn't be awake together in such close proximity for so much time without wanting to kill each other, which they could easily do, since they both had weapons.

The automatic cookstand went *DING!*

Removing the bowl of Bolkos-style stew, Jinto placed a second bowl on the filling stand. He readjusted the taste-concentration dial to "low," and hit the start button.

If Lafiel ate like a normal person, Jinto thought, *I could make both of our meals at the same time.*

The first time Jinto used the automatic cookstand, he made the mistake of giving Lafiel's food the same amount of seasoning as his. She barely tasted it before declaring it inedible.

The machine went *DING* again.

Jinto put the bowls and two cups of iced tea on a tray. He carried it toward the holo-broadcast receiver, which also served as their table. Jinto wondered if the people of Clasbul ever tried to watch the broadcasts while they ate or if that was considered rude.

"Here's the food," Jinto warned Lafiel, who was still watching the hologram.

The image of the broadcast had changed in Jinto's absence. Now, there was an androgynous figure with a classical orbital city (Baash) over her head.

"What's this?" Jinto set down the tray, distorting the image.

The broadcast's audio continued, unimpeded. ". . . with the objective of deep space investigation. Their interest was making living machines. Taking the technology of the time into consideration . . ."

"It's our origin," Lafiel explained indifferently.

"Origin? Of the Abh?" Jinto asked.

"Yes."

"And that is what they've done!" the woman shouted. "The Abh are not human! They are biological machines!"

"How terrible." Jinto reached for the machine's control buttons (Borsh). "Let's eat."

"Yeah."

"Free humans, we must put the Abh in their place! Machines serve humanity, not the other way around!" The skewed image and the woman's voice blipped off.

Quietly, Jinto and Lafiel took their food and began to eat.

In the middle of their meal, Lafiel spoke. "Jinto, about that broadcast . . ."

"I know," he assured her, "it's a bunch of garbage."

"No, it's not."

"Huh?"

"It's true. Our ancestors were built to be organic machines. You didn't know that?"

Jinto blinked; his Abh schooling did not prepare him for this.

Prior to the founding of the Empire, Bal Gureil was shrouded in mystery; in the year Before Empire (Bai Ruekot) one hundred twenty, an accident on the city-ship *Abriel* destroyed the ship's log—the only documentation of Abh history. Thus, Abh history before then was not in any history book anywhere.

Of course, the Abh knew their own history, but they were not keen to talk about themselves and especially not eager to divulge this odd information.

Now that he thought about it, Jinto recalled hearing a similar rumor during his Delktou days. At the time, it didn't make much of an impression on Jinto, because landers were always concocting wild rumors about the Abh.

"I didn't know that," Jinto finally answered.

"It's not in our writings; it's passed down orally through the generations."

"Apparently my father didn't know."

"Impossible. Lonyu Dreu Haider must have heard it at his title ceremony. It's known to all Abh."

"Huh. Well, he never told me." Perhaps his father thought it was absurd.

"Oh. Then, I'll tell you."

And Lafiel began to recount the true history of the Abh.

In ancient times, on planet Earth, there was a volcanic archipelago. Its inhabitants assimilated customs from all over and developed a unique culture, rich with tradition. However, globalization hit the islands hard. At first, the people welcomed these changes and prospered from them. Eventually, however, there was worldwide cultural confusion. Although the independent culture and language of the islands stuck out like a sore thumb, a small percentage of islanders had no intention of conforming. They refused to let the island's culture become "contaminated with imports."

Fed up, the small faction of purists left the planet.

They settled in one of Earth's established orbital cities, where they planned to rejuvenate their ancient culture. They changed their language; parts were reconstructed from its most basic words, parts were simply made up, and parts were resurrected from the annals of obsolescence.

The people were not happy in space and yearned to live on a Nahen again. Thus, they began to consider leaving the Solar System altogether. Mankind discovered its first Sord Loeza (this was before they even knew a Sord could be opened) and successfully utilized it to power a spaceship. This presented the possibility of traveling deeper into space.

However, the ex-islanders' aloofness isolated them from the rest of mankind, and Earth's other citizens neglected to include them in their deep-space immigration and exploration plans.

The seemingly unavoidable outcome was that the stubborn group plotted an independent space journey. They did not have a Sord Loeza; their only mode of transportation through the vacuum would have to be nuclear-fusion propulsion.

To compensate for their lack of efficient propulsion technology, the people manufactured superhuman crewmembers using forbidden science—human genetic engineering.

Selecting the best parts from the genes of their best people, they created thirty beings who, despite appearances, were not considered human. To further distinguish them from natural humans, the scientists gave them all unnatural, blue hair.

"This hair," Lafiel said, grabbing a lock of her recently blackened hair, "is the mark of a slave."

"So why," Jinto questioned, "are you so attached to it?"

"It reminds us of our liberation and also our original sin."

"Original sin?"

"The racial sin of the Abh."

After excessive training, the not-quite-humans piled into their low-speed ship, which promptly reached its aggravatingly slow maximum velocity. All they could do then was hope to stumble across a planet with enough hydrogen to power their return trip. No sane person would have gotten on the ship in the first place, but the prototype Abh had no frame of reference to gauge the absurdly slim odds of making it back alive.

At some point in the voyage, the Abh found a Sord Loeza. Gambling, they ate up most of their decelerating fuel trying to capture it. It paid off. Despite the limited resources aboard the craft, they retrofitted it for Sord Loeza propulsion and rocketed away.

Immediately after deviating from the proposed cruise schedule, the original Abh announced their secession from the mother city. Of course, they were in deep space, and there was no one around to acknowledge their rebellion, but that was irrelevant. The crew of twenty-nine wished to be an independent race.

"That's the racial sin? Seceding from the mother city?"

"No. That's just the setup."

While in the nearby star system, the Abh ancestors gathered enough resources to construct a bigger ship, which their increasing population desperately needed. The mother city's ship was merely an exploration vessel, but the Abh's new one was really grand—a veritable flying city.

There were no hard feelings; although coldly sent into space against impossible odds, the Abh did not hate the mother city. However, they did fear it. The thought of a disciplinary force coming from the mother city was always present in the back of their minds. In hindsight, the fear was completely illogical; the mother city didn't have the ability to send a disciplinary committee so deep into space—if they could do that, they never would have created the Abh in the first place.

The electronic databases aboard the ship enabled the Abh to build weapons and conduct militaristic training. The navigation officers who instituted the program of military conditioning were Lafiel's direct ancestors. The new city-ship was so massive and complicated to operate, and the number of people aboard was comparatively small, so there was simply not enough time to teach everyone how to perform every duty. That's when the Abh introduced their mentor-apprentice system of education, which eventually morphed into a system of hereditary education. Thus, for the most part, the different groups within the crew essentially became the different families of the Abh Empire.

As soon as they felt adequately prepared, the Abh undertook the mission of destroying the mother city.

"Harsh," judged Jinto.

"I said the same thing when my father told me," said Lafiel. "But if you lived in constant fear and thought you might live in fear forever and you had a chance to make it stop, would you do it?"

"I don't know. Tough question."

"Yeah, it's hard for us to say. Even my father couldn't really know, because he wasn't there either. I guess the fear was too great for our ancestors to bear, so they returned to the Solar System. And the rest is history."

It was a quick war.

By the time the Abh returned, the mother city had finally constructed its own Sord-propelled ships and sent whole generations of brave souls into space, having written off their genetic creations as lost.

If the Abh had known the diminished state of the mother city, they would not have been afraid, nor would they have journeyed through space to attack it.

When the Abh arrived, the mother city tried to convince the Abh that their ship's data had corrupted them. Seeing this as nothing more than an attempt to regain control over them, the Abh cut off negotiations and attacked the mother city.

Though the Abh were fewer in number, they were all soldiers with a wealth of weapons at their disposal. The citizens of the mother city hadn't been involved in any kind of war for a considerable time. Thus, there was hardly any resistance at all when the city-ship, a veritable interstellar fortress, charged in.

There were other nations in the Solar System, but none wanted to get involved for a number of reasons, the foremost being that the Abh were stronger than all the militaries in the Solar System put together.

By the time they were done, the mother city existed only as a conflagration, its inhabitants all dead.

"Once the forefathers accomplished their objective and saw the smoldering remains of the mother city, they realized the magnitude of their affection for it."

"Affection?" Jinto checked.

"Yes. It was their homeland, their culture. Culture was the whole reason the mother city existed and the reason our forefathers were born. And then it was gone. That is why the forefathers made it their primary objective to keep the culture alive."

"And that's still the Abh objective?"

"Yes. That was when they first called themselves 'Abh,' which in the language of the mother city means 'race of space or ocean.' Very appropriate for space nomads, don't you think?"

"Okay. But how does the enemy know all that?"

"It's not a secret. The Solar System's records are pretty cut-and-dried about what happened. Even many of the Frybar's Nahen know. Maybe your forefathers left the Solar System before mine returned."

Jinto nodded. "That makes sense. Because if my people knew the orbital city got obliterated, there would probably be at least a footnote in our history books."

Very seriously, Lafiel continued Jinto's education. "The Abh destroyed their own beloved homeland. That is our original sin. We protect our inherited culture. That is our mission. To be an Abh is to feel the burden of the mission and the sin. That's what Father said. And I think so, too."

Lafiel paused to study Jinto's reaction.

"You still want to be an Abh?" she asked.

"I don't have a choice." Jinto forced a smile. "I'm already an Abh, remember?"

"True," Lafiel agreed ambiguously.

Sighing, Jinto poked at what was left of his Bolkos-style stew.

"Housekeeping," said an unfamiliar woman, knocking on the door.

"Wait!" Jinto shouted.

But he was too late—the door was already open.

"Oops! Sorry to interrupt!" the woman apologized as she strode in with a new bedspread. She was tanned, with black hair and eyebrows. Jinto guessed she was probably in her thirties.

"Who are you?" Jinto's voice quavered.

"Isn't it obvious? I'm the room attendant. I'm here to change your sheets."

Stealing a glance at Lafiel, Jinto noticed she'd let her hair down in front, concealing her Frosh. He breathed a sigh of relief.

"But you've never changed the bedspread before," Jinto commented. "What brings you by all of a sudden?"

"Protocol, sir."

"We've been using that." He indicated the laundry slot in the wall, through which daily pickups and deliveries transpired.

"I'm sorry. There must have been a miscommunication then. As long as I'm here, I'll just put this in the bedroom."

"That's okay, I'll take care of it." Jinto tried to play it cool, even though he knew the Kreuno and Klanyu were in the bedroom, hidden under pillows, where this overeager woman would surely find them.

"It's really no trouble, sir. There's no reason a guest should have to—"

"Really, it's fine." Jinto interrupted boldly as he ran into the bedroom.

Emerging a moment later with the sheets under his arm, he shoved them at the confused but chipper woman.

The woman still clutched the clean sheets. "At least let me put these on for you."

"Not necessary, thanks. I'll do it myself. I'm very particular," he said politely.

"Oh, I see." Her expression indicated she thought Jinto was a weirdo. "Would you like me to take any dirty laundry with me?"

Doing his best to remain unflustered, Jinto handed her the laundry basket.

"My apologies." The woman bowed slightly.

"It's okay. Are you going to come back every day?"

She smiled. "Whatever the guest wants."

"Okay. If it's all the same to you, if you'll deliver it, I'd rather just do it myself."

"Very good."

"Say, how did you get in here?"

"I'm an employee. I have a key."

"There's no way to lock it from the inside?"

"Sir," she explained, "the inn must be able to enter in order to ensure the safety and well being of our guests."

Considering this, Jinto realized it made sense. "In the future, do you think you could possibly knock first?"

"I always do."

Although he wanted to protest, Jinto realized she had knocked—she just hadn't waited for an answer. He did not want to argue semantics with this madwoman; he wanted to remain on her good side.

The room clerk just stood there, staring at Jinto and Lafiel.

"Is there something else?" asked a confused Jinto.

The woman sighed. "It's kind of rude for me to ask this, sir, but are you familiar with the word 'Shifu'?"

This word certainly did not exist in Jinto's vocabulary. *What could she possibly want?* he wondered.

"How about 'gratuity'?" she angled.

"Oh, a tip!" yelled Jinto exuberantly, extremely pleased to figure out what she wanted. "Hang on, just a minute."

Jinto grabbed the little case he employed as a substitute wallet and pulled out a few coins, immediately turning them over to the expectant room clerk, who mentally counted them with a disapproving look.

Jinto added one more to the pile in her hand and the woman's smile returned.

"Might I make a suggestion, sir? For your convenience."

"Sure."

"In the future, you can simply put your Shifu in the laundry slot with your pickups. If you like. It is optional."

The way she said it, Jinto could tell it was not really optional.

"Oh, right. I'm sorry. I'm so absentminded," Jinto excused himself. "I'll try to make up for the missed days next time."

"Thank you, sir. You're a very understanding guest." She bowed. "Sorry to bother you."

As soon as she was gone, Jinto breathed an enormous sigh of release.

"What was that all about?" asked Lafiel.

"She came to ask for a tip."

Lafiel did not really understand this concept. She was certain they'd already paid for the room. Why did they also need to pay this woman?

Jinto gave up trying to explain it to her. He was comfortable in the knowledge that a set of rules had been established. If they failed to abide by the rules, the woman would come to sort it out, but if they abided, everything would be fine—he hoped.

13 Floating Car Discovery (Biryuukos Uuseil)

"You're a hundred percent sure it's the right one?" pressed Inspector Entoryua.

"There's no mistake," said the reporting detective. "It's got the same registration number, and there are traces of body fluids from all three of the victims in the car."

"Blood?"

"Semen."

"EUgh." Entoryua grunted, suddenly glad he wasn't in charge of that evidence. "I don't understand people who think the back seat of a car is a good place to get busy."

"Neither do I."

"And all three of them used the same car! Now that's just weird."

Shuddering, the men paused to consider the carnal atrocities the back seat had witnessed.

Entoryua quickly broke the silence. "I'm still more interested in investigating the crimes perpetrated by these 'victims' than finding out who stole their car."

"Forget about that," interrupted Kyte, who was apparently listening the whole time. "Any evidence of an Abh in the car?"

"We got more than fifty different hairs in there, so the genetic testing isn't finished yet," reported the detective.

"Then please get back to work right away."

The detective just stood there, staring blankly, until Entoryua gave him a look. Saluting, the detective ran off, presumably back to the lab.

Leaning on his command car, Entoryua lit another cigarette, fully aware how greatly it irritated Kyte.

Several detectives had made the trip from Luna Vega City to see the stolen car. They enjoyed dismantling autos to look for clues, but they weren't as fond of putting them back together afterward.

"We're hot on the trail," Kyte quipped.

"After only three days of looking," responded Entoryua sarcastically.

If these bastards weren't slowing us down, this wouldn't take so long. With our normal air patrols, we would have found the car in an hour, tops.

To his credit, Kyte did respond to Entoryua's request to grant passage permits to police vehicles. However, Kyte didn't have the authority to authorize this, and when he ran it by his superiors, they rejected it outright.

The incident made Entoryua wonder whether Kyte actually had any authority at all. But at least with Kyte accompanying them, the police had no trouble passing through checkpoints.

"What's the best course of action now, Inspector?" asked Kyte. "Comb all the homes in the area?"

Whoa there, big shot! thought Entoryua scornfully. *Looking through every house would require the entire Luna Vega police force, and it would still take months.*

"Hmm." Entoryua pretended to think. "This is Guzornyu, right? So I think we should call the Guzornyu City Police Department. It's their case now."

"Hand the case over?" Kyte shook his head in disbelief. "How can you be so indifferent? These criminals are dangerous and evil Abh. I know that until a couple days ago you were shouting 'long live Her Majesty the Empress' along with everyone else, but—"

"Actually," Entoryua butted in. "I don't even know Spunej's name."

"It is every man's right to know his government."

"If I wanted to know, I would. I just don't care."

"Political apathy is the enemy of democracy! By providing insufficient information, the Abh and the Rue Lef have made you all indifferent!"

"Don't talk about my ancestors like that."

Kyte paled, then coughed. "Your ancestors?"

"Yeah. Where did you think the name Entoryua came from? My relatives were Rue Lef just five generations ago. I think they were Sash in the Labule, but I don't know for sure. At any rate, life in space didn't suit them, so they settled here."

"Of course." Kyte shook off his temporary stupor. "Then you have a personal stake in the retribution!"

"I don't follow."

"Don't you see? Your family's been demoted from Lef to Sos! The ignominy!"

Smiling wryly, Entoryua calmly explained that Lef and Sos had the same standing, which troubled Kyte.

"You see," Entoryua continued, "the Frybar protects the rights of Lef, and the Semei Sos protects the rights of the Sos. So everyone's covered. It's just a matter of who's got your back. One of my best friends is Lef. It's not important to us."

"One of your friends?"

"Yeah. He's a plantation manager. Ever since you guys showed up, I can't seem to get in touch with him. I suspect he's probably in one of your internment camps . . . or 'democracy schools' or whatever."

"Of course. I don't know your friend personally, but I'm sure the democracy education—"

"There's one thing you just don't understand." Entoryua smiled through his disdain; though not as emotionally unsettling as the notorious "Abh Smile," it was a look that intimidated countless criminals. "And that's what it means to be a true friend."

Kyte gathered his courage. "You don't like working with me, do you?"

"It's starting to grow on me," the inspector claimed, while habitually tapping the dart gun (Kairia) in the holster on his hip.

"I must warn you," Kyte said gravely, "it's not a good idea to get on my bad side; I have unlimited arrest authority."

After surveying the scene for a moment, Entoryua determined that Kyte was completely outnumbered. "I'm sorry, I couldn't hear you over the noise of all these extremely loyal officers. You were saying something about unlimited arrest authority?"

Grinding teeth, Kyte stood his ground. "*My* men are all over this city, Inspector!"

"Funny, I don't see any."

Nervously, Kyte looked around.

Of course, Entoryua had no real intention of hurting Kyte. That would bring the wrath of a whole army down on his department, who were only packing Kairia. It simply wasn't a good idea.

"Hey, I'm just breaking your balls a little," Entoryua assured Kyte, patting him on the back with fatherly affection. "Maybe the joke doesn't translate. I thought you'd get a kick out of it, anyway."

"Oh. Ha. I get it." Cautiously, Kyte smiled. "I am not accustomed to the sense of humor around here, I guess."

"To each his own." Entoryua smiled, before grabbing Kyte and leaning in close to whisper in his ear. "Just remember, you're not welcome here. That'll help you understand more of the jokes." Grinning maliciously, Entoryua released the man.

After a moment, Kyte shook it off as though nothing had happened. "Okay, we'll implement the proposal and call Guzornyu City Police Department and have them send as many men as possible. Nonsmokers, preferably."

Grabbing the comms device from his belt, Entoryua dialed Aizan to clear the case transfer.

But, as Entoryua should have suspected, Aizan did not cooperate, mostly for political reasons; he did not want to jeopardize his standing with the occupation army.

Entoryua countered with the fact that if Guzornyu City PD failed to make an arrest, it would reflect poorly on *them,* not Aizan. Regardless, Aizan opposed it and told the inspector to keep working until he had the perpetrators in custody.

Using his classiest assortment of four-letter words, Entoryua insisted that a search would be monstrously difficult. Aizan hung up.

The inspector gave Kyte a thumbs-up. "That went well."

"In our world, asking to transfer a case like that is a direct violation of orders. This might be your swan song, Inspector."

"I'm not worried about it," Entoryua reassured him confidently.

In the small city of Luna Vega, Entoryua was something of a celebrity, known as one of the city's most prolific and fair policemen. If Entoryua got fired, Aizan would doubtless take heavy criticism. Aizan knew that as well as anyone.

Having waited patiently, the lead detective on the case took this opportunity to butt in. He held up a plastic evidence bag with a single hair in it. "The results are in, Inspector. This female hair is dyed—from its natural *blue*."

"If the inspector is busy," Kyte scolded, "report these things to me immediately!"

"No offense, Captain, but you're not in our chain of command." The lead detective stared at him coldly.

"I'm the same rank as the inspector," Kyte whined.

"I was not aware of that."

"Gentlemen! Let's focus on what's important," Entoryua interceded, grabbing the plastic bag. "We are hot on the trail."

"True." Kyte smoldered.

A split second before Entoryua realized he might have teased Kyte a little too much, his comms device rang. It was Aizan.

Apparently the superintendent had put in a call to Guzornyu City Police Department, and it had ended badly. Although they agreed to turn over any evidence they found regarding the case, they would not lend any men to the investigation.

The superintendent here must be more practical than Aizan, assessed Entoryua.

"So, Entoryua, just carry on with your duty as if you're acting alone," Aizan concluded.

Grunting affirmation, Entoryua disconnected the call. "We'll proceed on our own with the search," he relayed to Kyte.

"I see." The captain showed no expression at all. "We should call for a support unit."

"We won't get any more men from Luna Vega City Police," the inspector said bluntly, even though he knew Aizan would do whatever it took to send men upon Kyte's request. Aizan would pull the station's accountants from their desks if necessary.

"No," corrected Kyte, "from my unit. I'll call it in."

Using the need for more men as a pretext, Kyte would bring in some allies to make himself more comfortable, Entoryua figured. It was a natural and wise course of action.

"Oh. Yes, it looks like no matter how many men we can get, it won't seem like enough," he agreed passively. Maybe he would convince Kyte that they should split up, which would enable both men to work unencumbered by their resentment of each other.

Nodding, Kyte bought his wrist communications device to his mouth and began to speak into it grandiosely. Although he could not understand a word of Kyte's language, the captain couldn't hide his anger and disappointment. Entoryua knew the outcome of the call.

A good man at his core, Entoryua felt sorry for Kyte. "Why is everyone so glum around here? Somewhere, someone must be hogging all the happiness."

"Yes," mumbled Kyte. "So, how do we proceed now, Inspector?"

"Well, with the numbers we've got, it's pretty much impossible to comb through all the houses, so we should start with the nearby hotels and inns, then branch out from there."

"This is going to take a while, isn't it?"

"Yeah." The inspector flicked the remains of a cigarette through the air. "Unless they were dumb enough to check into one of the hotels around here."

"Resistance is useless!" a man shouted, effectively snapping Jinto out of his holo-broadcast stupor.

Four men advanced, their Ribwasia drawn. They made it known that they were not afraid to zap Jinto rigid if he moved so much as an inch the wrong way.

"Who are you and what do you want?" Jinto responded.

"What do we look like?" demanded the shortest of the men.

"P-police?" Jinto sweated.

Clad in yellow and green uniforms, the men didn't really resemble any police Jinto had ever seen. But then again, Clasbul was home to the worst fashions in the universe, so Jinto didn't put it past its police to also look ridiculous.

"Where's the Abh girl?" demanded the short guy.

With his hands in the air, Jinto played dumb. "You must have the wrong room; it's just me in here."

Lafiel was still in the bedroom. *If I can just keep them out of there,* Jinto hoped.

"She's probably in there sleeping," the little guy didn't buy it, "like any sane person. What are you doing up at this hour? You're ruining our plans!"

Am I supposed to apologize? wondered Jinto.

The short man instructed a very burly, dark-skinned man to go take a look in the bedroom. Nodding, the massive man went toward the door. A second guy—a skinny guy with a recently-shaved head—followed.

"Stop!" Temporarily forgetting the paralysis gun, Jinto ran at the big guy.

As if swatting a fly, the huge man deflected Jinto with a wave of his arm, sending the young man tumbling backward. After landing in a crumpled heap, Jinto staggered to get back up but stopped when he came face-to-face with the barrel of a gun.

"I acknowledge your courage," said the short man as he burrowed the gun into Jinto's forehead, "but if you move again, I'll shoot you."

"Are you here to arrest us?"

"Something like that."

"What does that mean?"

"Shut up." The small man's attention turned to the larger man. "What are you waiting for, an invitation?"

Seizing the opportunity, Jinto grabbed the small man's arm, wrestling him to the floor. In the fray that ensued, Jinto managed to twist the man's wrist pretty hard.

"Ow!" The little man dropped the Ribwasia.

The instant Jinto reached for the fallen gun, two bodies pounced on him. Luckily for Jinto, neither one belonged to the enormous man.

"Crap!" Jinto said, his face mashed into the floor, a his limbs all held firmly in place.

"Hold him there!" commanded the small man as he picked up the gun.

"Shouldn't we stun him?!" suggested the young-looking bottle-blond sitting on Jinto's back.

"What, and carry him the whole way? Use your head, man!"

"But, Undertaker—"

"Call me 'Police Chief,' dumbass!"

"Yes, sir, Police Chief."

I don't think these guys are really policemen, thought Jinto. *But who are they then? They're definitely not the occupation army.*

Putting a halt to Jinto's thought processes, the little man shoved his gun up against the back of Jinto's head. "I know you're very loyal to that girl. And I want you to walk out of here under your own power, I really do. But I will shoot you if I have to." The man paused before deciding he wanted to add to his threat. "Ever been shot with a Ribwasia? Just because you can't move doesn't mean you can't feel it burn."

"You're not really the police, are you?" Jinto asked.

The skinny man whistled. "I like this guy, asking a question like that in his situation. Incredible!"

"Who cares?!" shouted "Police Chief" Undertaker. He looked at the large man. "Get a move on, Daswani! We don't have all day!"

Nodding wordlessly, Daswani opened the bedroom door. He only took one step into the bedroom before he stopped in his tracks and backed out of the room, slowly and deliberately.

At first, Jinto didn't understand what the man was doing, but then Lafiel emerged, yawning, a Klanyu clutched in her hand. Her Frosh peeked out through her sleep-mussed hair, glinting conspicuously.

Compared to Lafiel's menacing-looking, flesh-searing Klanyu, the men's Ribwasia were just toys, both in appearance and damage potential.

"An Abh!" the young man said reverently. "There really was one."

Daswani backed all the way into the wall.

Nobody moved.

Finally, Police Chief broke the silence with his thickly accented, but unexpectedly competent, Baronh.

"Throw down your gun, Abh, unless you want us to hurt your friend here. From this close, a Ribwasia can kill, you know."

"If he dies," Lafiel said in a monotone, "so will all of you. In case you feel like testing me, you ought to know that I'm extremely irritated right now."

"Understandably so," mumbled Undertaker. "Nobody likes to be woken up."

Sensing that no one was listening, the young man snapped, "There are four of us! You can't fight us all."

"Try me." Lafiel's eyes narrowed.

Instinctively, the bottle-blond started to turn his Ribwasia toward Lafiel. Before he could even think about what he was doing, Lafiel fired. The laser beam struck the man's weapon, which instantly absorbed the beam's heat.

"Ouch!" The young man dropped the glowing-hot Ribwasia.

Seeing this, the huge guy thought it was a good opportunity to make his move, drawing his gun on Lafiel. Before he could squeeze the trigger however, a Klanraj struck the weapon. Enduring the burn, he pulled the trigger.

Nothing happened of course; Lafiel's laser had melted the gun's interior.

Lafiel fired two quick shots that grazed the man's sides.

Daswani gulped. "Don't shoot anymore," he said, tossing his gun to the floor.

"Marksmanship is one of my many talents," Lafiel began quietly. "Normally, I don't miss like that. I must be tired. I'm awake now, though, if anyone wants to try again."

A heavy silence fell on the room. The short man sweated profusely.

In the ruckus, the two other men had let go of Jinto's limbs, but they hadn't let him up, so he was still squished to the floor. Even more distressing, the short man kept his gun firmly pressed into the back of Jinto's head.

"Hey, guys," Jinto said, "maybe you ought to let me up."

After giving Jinto the nastiest of looks, Undertaker contemplated his Ribwasia and Lafiel's Klanyu. Finally, the man dropped the gun.

The two other men liberated Jinto from his spot on the floor.

He rolled over to Lafiel, then stood beside her. "I'm glad you reconsidered," Jinto said sincerely.

"Reconsidered what?" asked Police Chief. The man's expression, however, seemed to indicate that he understood Lafiel had originally intended to shoot to kill.

"We understand each other," asserted Jinto.

"Agreed. Understanding is always important." The man stretched his arms to his sides. "Welcome to Clasbul, from the official welcoming committee!"

"I spoke too soon," muttered Jinto.

"Jinto," Lafiel said, "we're leaving. Go get our stuff together. I'll keep an eye on them."

"Know what? I'm going to get our stuff now," Jinto declared as if it were his idea. He went into the bedroom and returned quickly with the duffel bag in one hand and his Klanyu in the other.

"Shall we?" he proposed to Lafiel.

"We shall." She turned to the disappointed men. "All of you, into the bedroom. Now."

"Hold on," Undertaker begged. "We're *friends*."

"Who happened to barge in with guns drawn!" Jinto exclaimed.

"Let me explain. Don't you want to know who we really are?"

"Not really," Jinto said.

"Despite your youth, you're not curious? Curiosity is the source of progress!" rebuked Undertaker.

"I don't care whether you're guerrillas or undertakers or birdwatchers," Jinto said coldly.

"I'm the only undertaker here," asserted the small man proudly.

"What, was business slow this week, so you came to rustle up some bodies?"

"Never mind that," Lafiel interrupted. "Just get into the bedroom already."

Goading them with the gun, Lafiel ushered the men to the entrance of the bedroom. She heard a door open—the door to the hallway.

What now? she thought.

Tense, Jinto raised his weapon.

The room attendant from the previous day entered. "You guys can't do anything right," she reprimanded the four men.

"You *know* these goons?" Jinto asked.

"I'm in charge of this ramshackle crew." Her Baronh was even better than Jinto's. "Don't worry, though, I'm not armed."

"You're not an employee at this hotel?"

"No."

"So the whole 'Shifu' thing was a big charade!"

"Not entirely," the woman objected. "You guys have quite a reputation among the staff here for failing to tip."

Slightly embarrassed, Jinto looked at the floor.

Smiling in Lafiel's direction, the woman said, "Miss Abh, you've missed some spots in the back; you can't afford to be so hasty with the hair dye."

"Thanks," said Lafiel sarcastically. "But you're still going in the bedroom with these guys."

"Please, hear us out."

"First, get over there in line with these guys."

"Can't be too cautious, I guess." The woman obeyed. Now, the five intruders stood in a row and Lafiel could keep an eye on all of them at the same time.

"Why do I feel like we're in front of a firing squad?" grumbled the small man.

"It's okay, Undertaker," assured the skinny man. "If she wanted to kill us, we'd already be dead."

"Let us introduce ourselves. I'm Marca," said the fake hotel employee.

"Call me Undertaker. That's not my real name, of course," added the diminutive man.

"Just call me Minh," said the thin man. For the first time, Jinto noticed Minh's moustache, which was bleached on one side and dyed red on the other.

"Bill. Everyone in town calls me Bill Tobashiya," said the young-looking man.

"Daswani," offered the huge guy.

After that, they stood silently.

It suddenly dawned on Jinto that they were waiting for him to introduce himself. "I'm sorry," he said, "I don't feel like telling you who we are."

"No matter," Marca said confidently. "The names on the register will do, Jinto Sai. And Lena Sai, is that right?"

"Yes."

"Then that's what we'll call you. Jinto seems to be your real name, at least."

This Marca lady must have sharp ears, Jinto thought. *Somehow, she must have heard Lafiel call me by name.*

"Lena isn't an Abh name, though," Minh puzzled.

Jinto said, "You don't need to know her real name."

"How about a last name? She looks like she has a recognizable name. Maybe she's even from Loebeje Sufagnaum."

"Maybe she is, maybe she isn't. We aren't saying. We still don't know who you really are, or what you're doing here."

"Oh, right," Marca said. "We're members of the Anti-Empire Clasbul Front."

"Anti-Empire? It doesn't really help your standing with us, if you hate the Abh."

"Oh," she explained, "we don't hate the Abh in particular, Jinto. We just want to have our own spaceship for trade and exploration."

"The Frybar would never allow that!" he insisted.

"Yes, hence our resistance."

"You're going against the Frybar . . ."

"It wouldn't do any good for us to fight the birdwatchers, would it?"

"You know that we are people of the Frybar, right?"

"Of course. She is clearly an Abh."

"And yet you're not our enemies." Jinto concluded cynically.

"Absolutely."

"Okay." Jinto nodded, more in recognition of their true objective than in agreement with Marca. He turned back to Lafiel. "Good story, huh? Shall we?"

"Wait! That's not all of it."

"It's getting too complicated for me," Jinto complained.

"We're not talking to you anyway, Lef," asserted Bill. "Marca's speaking to the Abh lady, so be quiet, servant."

Though miffed, Jinto held his tongue. Even if he told them he was Sif, they probably wouldn't believe him. And even if they did believe it, that wouldn't necessarily be a good thing.

"His words are my words. Don't look down on him," Lafiel said.

After hearing that, Bill appeared temporarily jealous of Jinto.

"Now tell us—what is your objective?" Lafiel got to the point.

Grinning grotesquely, Undertaker said, "We want to take you hostage."

"Jinto, you were right," Lafiel stated. "It's time for us to go."

"Good idea." Jinto began to back away slowly, keeping his gun trained on the intruders the whole time. "Thanks for stopping by, guys. Really nice to meet you all."

"Please, wait!" Marca smacked Undertaker upside the head. "This idiot misspoke."

"My arm's getting tired," Lafiel complained. "So make it quick."

"You two won't make it in this world," Marca said frantically. "You stick out like camels at a swim meet. But, if you let us 'capture' you, we can hide you until the Abh return."

"Gee, that's awfully nice of you," said Jinto warily. While nothing would benefit them more than cooperative locals, he didn't think they ought to take help from the Anti-Empire front. "What's in it for you?"

"A bartering chip for negotiations," Undertaker said as if it were the most obvious thing in the world.

"Shut up, big mouth!" Marca said. "As Undertaker crudely put it, we want to negotiate with the Empire, but have no leverage."

"Your request will be denied," clarified Lafiel. "Even if I were Spunej Erumita herself, the Frybar cannot . . ." she trailed off.

Jinto understood the unsaid; the Abh did not accommodate hostage takers. Period. Instead, the kidnappers would receive whatever retribution the Abh deemed proportional to the perceived cowardice of taking hostages.

Jinto nudged Lafiel to get her attention. "Let's play along," he whispered, "and let them think they can negotiate."

"You want to lie to them?" Lafiel asked, disgusted.

"No, it's not lying," Jinto explained, "because they already had this preposterous idea in their heads. We just won't correct them."

"Valid." She hovered on the edge of saying something else.

"Let's let them dream for now," Jinto jumped in. "It won't be our fault when their expectations go awry."

"That might make it worse when they find out we're useless as hostages. What's to stop them from killing us then?"

"We won't be real hostages. Trust me."

"You're running out of time, you know." Sensing a chance to make her case, Marca resumed her rapid-fire speech. "It won't be long before the occupation army finds you—you don't exactly blend in, dyed hair or not."

"Okay," Jinto said to silence her. "We'll go with you, but under a few conditions."

"The hostage is setting the conditions!" Undertaker said incredulously. "Maybe you're not familiar with the concept."

"Shut up, idiot! If you guys hadn't screwed it up, then we wouldn't have to beg them to be our hostages with guns in our faces."

"Maybe you should have done it yourself, Marca." Undertaker was not repentant.

"You're supposed to be the big, tough goons!" Marca yelled. "I'm just a 'feeble woman,' remember?"

Jinto said, "Will you hear our conditions or not?"

"Go ahead," said Marca.

"Number one: we're keeping the weapons."

"Armed hostages?" scoffed Undertaker.

"Keep your tmouth shut, Undertaker! What else?"

"You cannot separate us unless we ask you to."

"Fine. That it?"

"Lastly, we want to be informed of everything in advance. You'll tell us where we're going, what actions you're going to take next, et cetera."

"Fine," accepted Marca. "Now, let's get out of here."

When Marca swallowed all the conditions without hesitation, Jinto wished he'd asked for more.

"Wait, she has to change first." Jinto pointed to Lafiel, who was still wearing the sleepwear provided by the inn.

"No, I don't," Lafiel protested. "I like this outfit better than that thing you got me."

"What do you think?" Jinto asked Marca.

She shrugged. "They look like regular pajamas, but it's not very common to see people wearing them outdoors."

"See?" Jinto handed her the dress. "Get changed."

"Don't treat me like a child!" Lafiel stomped off.

"Weirdest Sif and Rue Lef I've ever seen," remarked Bill.

Daswani shrugged agreement.

"One more question," said Jinto. "Your whole plan is based on the assumption that the Frybar recovers this world. What if the Frybar doesn't strike back?"

"You really think the Abh would ever give up?" Undertaker stared at Jinto. "That's the craziest damn thing I've heard all year!"

At that very moment, an Abh Byr traveled through Fath near the Yuunyu 303 Star System.

The Abh were relieved; Iliish Kingdom and its Sord were a mere six thousand Gedolel from Loebhynu Sufagnaum. A Pelia could rip through six thousand Gedolel in about five hours. Even something as slow as an Isath could cover that distance in about seventy hours.

The fleet's flagship (Glaga) was a Resii called *Keildij*; an absolute beast of a ship with a two-story Gahorl. At the highest point on the ship, the admiral (Frode) named Trife Borje-Yubudeil Remseil paced nervously around the bridge command seat (Gahorl Grawl).

Unusual for an Abh, he was a stout man with dark green hair. His light-brown face was fiercely sharp, like a hawk's. When he spoke, the Trife family trait (Wariit) of highly-developed canines became visible and he resembled a wolf. Bird or beast, one thing was clear: the man was unquestionably severe, seemingly born for battle.

Trife's aides (Sperush), consisting of twelve staff officers (Kasalia), one adjutant (Lukia), and many officers from headquarters (Katboth), crammed into the bridge to watch their excited C.O.

Three crest banners hung in a triangle on the wall behind the command seat (Glahareribash), in which Trife ought to have been sitting. The crest at the apex was the Rue Nigla—the Gaftonosh. Below it to the left, there was the Lalbryubu Peace Protection Office's (Shuteyum Lalbryubu's) banner, which featured an eight-headed dragon eternally engaged in a skirmish with a lightning bolt. On the right, a perk of high rank, hung the Trife family's crest banner, called the Grieving Pheasant (Ktesh). Only commanders of the partial fleet (Lesheik Jadbyr) or higher were allowed the privilege.

"Lonyu," the chief of staff (Was Kasaler) said to get Trife's attention, "Resii *Adoras* sent the latest diagram of the situation."

Unlike his superior, Was Kasaler Kahyuul Borto-Satek Jarluk Lemeish Shewas was slim. His hair was a more typical shade of blue; his appearance was handsome, but not extremely different from that of lander men. His eyes were always somewhat droopy, as if he needed to take a nap.

"Oh?" Trife nodded. "Let's see it."

"Yes, sir." Kahyuul motioned to a subordinate, and a hologram of Fath floated into view.

Space-time particles (Supflasath) continually flowed outward from the central, high-density area of Sordlash Elukufar. Eventually, these Supflasath collided with those erupting from the space-time volcanoes (Kiigaf) near Sord Sufagnaum in Speish Lomata.

It would be difficult for Labule Flasath to enter that high-activity area, especially if they had to dodge mines. Thus, that area was this battle's high ground. Naturally, there was a large number of enemy Flasath congregating there, in the ideal position to defend Sord Sufagnaum.

"The enemy knows we're coming," Kahyuul stated. "They've made contact with our fleet."

"Guessing from the mass here, we're dealing with three half fleets. Not much at all." Trife smiled; he'd expected much more opposition than that.

"Is that their whole army?"

"Probably. I know if I were calling the shots for the enemy army, I'd go for it with everything at my disposal."

"Do we have any evidence, or are we just acting on gut instinct now?"

"Regrettably," Kahyuul admitted, shaking his head. "The Spaude Rirrag didn't catch the invasion before it started, so it's impossible to know the exact extent of their troop strength."

"Spaude Rirrag?" Trife repeated, annoyed. "Those incompetents couldn't catch a stray cat!"

"That's a little harsh, Lonyu," suggested Comms Staff Officer (Kasalia Drokia) Roibomowas Nasotoryua, who had transferred just days earlier from the Military Command Headquarters' Spaude Rirrag. She knew firsthand how much effort the people working in Intelligence put forth.

"Perhaps," conceded Trife. He paced some more.

The intelligence officers were not as inept as Trife imagined; he just held personal resentment toward the Seif Spauder Rirrag, Frode Kashunanshu, due to a feud over a girl back in their Kenru Lodair days.

Kashananshu is spiteful and incompetent; it's a cruel joke to give a guy like that such an important job. Regardless, I shouldn't criticize all his subordinates, who have mostly done a pretty decent job, Trife thought.

"My apologies," the Glaharerl began. "The bunch at Spaude Rirrag has done excellent work tracking cats!"

After it sank in for a moment, almost everyone seemed satisfied with this half-apology. Nasotoryua smoldered momentarily, but held her tongue.

Now, Trife pushed Intelligence Bureau matters out of his mind, *on to more important things, such as what do we do now?*

There were seven half fleets (Jadbyr) under his command: Assault Half Fleets (Jadbyr Ashal) Byuuldef, Rokeil, Wakapeil, and Kitiil; Strike Half Fleet (Jadbyr Vortout) Bask Gamlyuf; Recon Half Fleet (Jadbyr Usem) Futuune; and Support Half Fleet (Jadbyr Dikporleil) Ashmatosh.

On top of that, Trife had a few independent squadrons (Sov Raglaze) with temporary land forces and their direct-command vessel (Glabauria) at his disposal. All in all, Byr Trife comprised almost twenty-one hundred ships.

Never enough, Trife maligned internally.

However, seven half fleets were all that the Peace Protection Office had granted Trife after learning of the attack in Loebehynu Sufagnaum.

The first objective was reconnaissance; they were to determine the size and strength of the enemy's troops and, more importantly, their intentions. But seven Jadbyr seemed excessive for simple recon. All Trife would need for that was the Jadbyr Usem Futuune.

Conversely, if the true objective was to recapture Loebehynu Sufagnaum, then his current fleet size seemed too small.

I must've drawn an unlucky lottery, Trife determined.

As one of four Peace Protection Office Vice-Commanders (Roiglaharerl), Trife knew he could be called upon to lead a fleet in times of war. Although he had no ships under his control during peacetime, he now found himself at the helm of a massive squad. He secretly wished for any of the three men who'd been passed over to take his place.

The fact that they had not yet encountered any enemy troops made Trife exceedingly nervous. That meant that the enemy's strength lurked in Loebehynu Sufagnaum. Even if the force were small, it would be concentrated.

"We can win," Trife told his Was Kasaler.

"True," he agreed, "but it's just an assumption that all the enemy's force will be there."

"I don't like fighting on assumptions."

"Shall we withdraw then? Or wait for support?"

"No, let's forget being cautious," Trife decided, flinging his arms up in the air, "and recapture Marquis Sufagnaum's territory!"

"Yes, sir!" The Kasalia all clicked their heels in unison.

"Kahyuul, how long will it take?"

"First, we need to sort a couple things out," the Was Glaharerl said.

"Such as?"

"Should we include complete destruction of the enemy in our strategic objective?"

Eager to offer an opinion, Operations Staff Officer (Kasalia Yokuskurot) Bomowas Shuliil spoke up. "We could employ a turning pincer movement."

Trife thought it over; it was certainly an appealing idea.

The turning pincer movement was a pretty showy maneuver that involved sending half of the fleet to the enemy's rear to cut off their escape. Meanwhile, the other half approached from the front and they attacked from both flanks. If successful, the enemy would be decimated.

Given the circumstances, it was hard to think of a way this could fail. The Byr outnumbered the enemy two to one. Even if the Abh lost an individual battle, they would still win the war.

Also, Trife had the Jadbyr Usem Futuune. Most people thought of a recon half fleet as being completely impotent, a barely-armed support unit. In actuality, it was much more than that.

The recon half fleet was equipped to gather information from hostile territory by any means necessary. When an Alek or Gel got in a Jadbyr Usem's way, its Resii simply destroyed them.

Thus, the battle strength of a recon half fleet was equivalent to five normal half fleets. Many people thought the entire Labule arsenal should consist of recon half fleets, but they were monstrously expensive to operate, so they weren't commonly deployed.

As it stood, Trife had a heavily armed cavalry galloping through space at his command. No unit could possibly employ a pincer movement more effectively than a Jadbyr Usem.

After considering the attack for a moment, Trife finally abandoned the notion, though his desire to do it lingered. "Unfortunately, our objective isn't battle. We are merely to recapture Loebehynu Sufagnaum. Even though victory is certain, we can't afford to lose vessels in a profitless battle."

"B-but—" Shuliil argued.

"Enough already. Please don't tempt me!"

"Yes, sir."

"So we'll continue to advance and intimidate the enemy?" checked Kahyuul.

"For now, that's the plan." Oh, how Trife wished he could justify the pincer movement. "We'll probably scare them off if we advance slowly in a diagonal line formation."

"Roger. I'll draw up some specs."

"How long until we can get started?"

"What do you want to do with the Resii out on recon duty?"

"We'll meet up with them on the way," Trife said.

"We should be able to depart in about two hours."

"Make it one."

"Got it."

Maybe I should have said fifteen minutes, Trife regretted.

"Good. If I don't have a detailed strategic plan in my hands in one hour, I'll be extremely disappointed."

"Yes, sir."

As the Kasalia left the operations room (Shirsh Yokuskurot), Trife finally took his place in the Glahareribash.

In exactly one hour, Kahyuul handed Trife a comprehensive set of course plans and line of battle ranks.

Trusting the judgment of his Was Kasaler implicitly, Trife approved the plans after a cursory glance.

"Gentlemen," he announced. "We will now recapture Loebehynu Sufagnaum. Sadly, there may not be a battle. However, if the need arises, I expect you to fight beautifully. Sathoth Frybareri! Now launch!"

Upon his command, two thousand vessels fired up their Asort simultaneously.

To be continued in
Seikai: Crest of the Stars:
Return to a Strange World

Appendix:
Abh Weights and Measures

The greatest similarity between Abh and Earth measurements has to do with time. One Abh year equates to three hundred and sixty-five days; one day is twenty-four hours; one hour is sixty minutes; and one minute is sixty seconds.

The difference, however, is that the Abh do not rely on fixed stars or calendars to mark their years, so there are no leap years nor leap seconds.

Other basic Abh units are also derived from prehistoric Earth measurements. The Abh "meter" is related to the circumference of the earth, and their gram is the mass of a cubic centimeter of water under Earth's gravity.

Of course, the Abh have their own words for these concepts and measurements, with their own complex system of prefixes, which change according to the ten thousands' place.

Neglecting time (see above), the basic units of measurement are as follows:

Length: Daj = centimeter (cm)
Mass: Boh = Gram (g)

The following prefixes can change the amount.

[Scale]	[Prefix]	[Length]	[Mass]
10^{20}	Dorial-	1000 trillion km	100 trillion t
10^{16}	To-	100 billion km	10 billion t
10^{12}	Zesa-	10 million km	1 million t
10^{8}	Se-	1000 km	100 t
10^{4}	Wes-	Wes-	10 kg
1		100 m	1 g
10^{-4}	Shes-	1 micrometer	0.1 mg
10^{-8}	Sowafu-	1 Angstrom	0.01 microgram
10^{-12}	Kos-	10 Y (Yukawa)	
10^{-16}	Peta-	0.001 Y	

Thus, three Zesdaj would be thirty million kilometers. Eight hundred Wesboh would be eight metric tons.

The Abh also use light-seconds and light-years as units of measurement, so it is rare for them to use this system to describe lengths greater than Zesdaj.

They also have a complex unit system based on Planck length and mass.

Naturally, Plane Space, which is governed by different laws of physics than normal space, requires a different system of measurements. In Plane Space, the common measurement is the Imperial nautical mile (Kedlairl) and the Imperial knot (Digrl).

One Kedlairl is defined as "the distance a space-time with a mass of one Seboh (100 tons) in perfect motion travels in one second of Flasath time."

The Digrl is "the speed at which it is possible to travel one Kedlairl in one hour of Flasath time."

Notes from the Editor and Fan Consultants:

As Morioka-sensei has stated no rules for upper or lower case Barohn, please note that all Abh words in Romanized form are capitalized.

All silent letters are removed. In most cases, vowels are pronounced as they would be in Italian.

Changes to the endings of certain nouns (pertaining to direction, possession, etc.) are due to the Baronh noun declension system. Example: The nominative Lodair**l** becomes Lodair when used in the possessive.

The letter **C** always makes a hard consonant sound, so **C** becomes **K** in this text.

There is no **J** in authentic Baronh, but for phonetic purposes, an **Ï** becomes **J**, and the soft 'ge' sound (like in 'page') is spelled 'jhe' (as in 'Ruejhe').

Unlike Japanese, Baronh has a clear distinction between the letters **R** and **L**. A semi-rolled **R** is spelled "rl" here.

There is no **W** in authentic Baronh, but for phonetic purposes, an **Ü** becomes **W**.

The letter **Y** is never used as a vowel or given its own individual syllabic emphasis.

In written Barohn, there's a distinction between a voiced "th" and an unvoiced "th." For the sake of simplicity, we did not make the distinction in written Baronh here.

For more information, do a web search for "Baronh" and visit fan sites like the following:

For pronunciation rules:
http://www.geocities.com/gatewaytoseikai/1_en.html

For characters' names, military ranks, culture, history, etc.:
http://www.geocities.com/Tokyo/Shrine/4777/Seikai/seikai.html

A Baronh-Japanese Only Dictionary:
http://dadh-baronr.s5.xrea.com/doc/baronhdic-1.html#A

For a comprehensive overview of the *Seikai* universe:
http://www.abhnation.com/

If you read Japanese, try the two Reader Guides entitled *Seikai no Monshou Dokuhon* (1999) and *Seikai no Senki Dokuhon* (2001).

Glossary

A

Agaim	To kill
Aith	Country, nation
Alpha	Abh control tiara
Alm Belysega	Control room chief officer
Alm Goneudo	Head Housekeeper
Apezm	Sash clip
Apyuf	Seat belt
Areik	Battle-line ship
Arnej	Orbital tower
Arosh	The Imperial capital (Lakfakalle)
Asertaf	State of Illumination
Asort	Propulsion flames; engine fires

B

Baash	City
Bai Ruekot	Before Empire
Baikok	Antimatter fuel tank
Baish	Antimatter fuel
Banzorl Garyuk	Household rooms
Bar Lepenu	Pride of the Abh
Bar Seida	Arms of the Abh
Bar Sif	Abh nobility
Basev	Agricultural lands
Baud	Round door
Bei	Palace
Belysega	Air Traffic Control
Belysega Lyumusko	The Lyumex's control
Bene Lodair	Pilot Trainee
Bes	Dock
Bidaut	Spaceport
Bidaut Alsa	Trade ports
Biiz	Propellant

Bomowas	Hecto-Commander
Borje Sufagnaum	Viscount Safugnoff's family
Borl Paryuun	Viscount of Paryuunyu
Borl Sufagnaum Daglei	Daglei, Viscount of Safugnoff
Borsh	Control buttons
Borskor Sufagnaum	Viscount Safugnoff's territory
Bosnal	Military officer
Bosnal Labule	Star Force Officer
Bowazebuku	Memory hive
Bruvoth Gos Suyun	Four Nations Alliance
Bynkerl	Controller
Bynkerlseraj	Control functionality
Byr	Fleet
Byr Drok Lonid Sufagnaum	Communication Fleet Safugnoff Base

C

D

Dadjocs	Battle in normal space
Daemon	Standard gravity
Dath	Normal space
Datykirl	Computer crystal
Daush	Long robe
Daushasairl	Clothier; dresser
Diafsairl	Bedroom duty official
Dib	Airtight adhesive
Digrl	Imperial knot
Dobroria	Ascent-descent tube
Doh	Rubies
Dreu	Count(ess)
Dreuhynu Bisurel	Count Bisure's territory
Dreuhynu Gogam	Count Gogarf's territory
Dreuhynu Haidar	Count Hyde's territory
Dreuhynu Vorlak	Count Vorlash's territory
Dreujhe	Count's family
Druejhe Haidar	Count Hyde's family

E

Eifu	Computer network
Elukufa	Milky Way
Erumita / Erumiton	Your Majesty

F

Fal Lonyu	My Excellent Lord
Fal Sif	My lord, my master
Faneb	Young man
Fapyut	Sovereign
Fapyut Semei Sos	Territorial citizens' government
Faroll Sok	Control layer
Fasanzoerl	Imperial family
Fath	Plane space
Fazia Har	Shipbuilding Engineer
Febdashos	History of Baron Febdash's territory
Feia	His / Her / Your Highness
Feia Dusan	Your Highness Dusanyu
Feia Lalt Kryuv	His Highness King Klyuve
Feia Lartneir	Her Highness the Queen
Feia Loran	His Highness the King, my father
Fek	Kingdoms
Fek Irik	Iriish Kingdom
Flarf	Necklace
Flasath	Time-space bubble
Flasatia	Time-space creation engine
Frelia	Ground car
Frode	Admiral
Frokaj	Alpha spacial recall device to "feel" space
Frosh	Space sense organ in an Abh's forehead
Frybar	Empire (n.) or Imperial (adj.)
Frybar Gloer Gor Bari	Humankind Empire of Abh
Fryum Neg	Daughter of love
Ftiainyu	Amber

G

Ga Fek	Eight Kingdoms
Gaf Laka	Tall Mountain

Gaftonosh	Eight-headed dragon, symbol of the Abh Empire
Gahorl	Ship's bridge
Gahorl Grawl	Bridge command seat
Gal Guraw	Crest banner(s)
Gareur	Association
Gareurl Faziar Deiwim	Planet modification engineering association(s)
Garish	Orbital mansion
Geiku Skofarimeil	Embassy
Geinyu	Synthetic resin
Gel	Assault ship(s)
Glabauria	Direct-command vessels
Glaga	Flagship
Glagaf	HQ
Glahareribash	Command seat
Glaharerl Rue Byrer	Imperial Fleet Commander-in-Chief
Goh Ramgokotot	The age of space wandering
Golkia	Successor
Gono	Pressurized suit(s)
Gooheik	Control glove
Gor Putarloth	Time-space fusion
Gosnoh	No abnormalities; everything A-OK
Gosuk	Vassal(s)
Gosuk Ran	Honorable Vassal

H

Hoksath	Mine(s)

I

Isath	Transport / supply ship(s)

J

Ja Fad	Map of Plane Space
Jadbyr	Fleet section
Jadbyr Ashal	Assault Half Fleet
Jadbyr Dikporleil	Support Half Fleet
Jadbyr Usem	Recon Half Fleet
Jadbyr Vortout	Strike Half Fleet

Jarluk Dreu Haidar	Count Hyde's son
Jarluk Lemeish Shewas	Kilo-Commander
	Count's son Lemeish
Jath Syroegna Le Klasbyr	Snail with silver twig
	(Sosie's family crest)
Jeish	Memory sheet
JothAntimatter	fuel factories
Joth Lokeutona	Fuel factory #11
Jotmsei Ryurdauwa	Carbon crystal fiber spindle

K

Kairia	Dart gun
Kareug	Rope ladder
Kasalia	Staff officer, Advisor
Kasalia Drokia	Communications Staff Officer
Kasalia Yokuskurot	Operations Staff Officer
Kasarl	Brethren
Kasarl Gereulak	"Kin of the Stars" (the Abh)
Kasorvia	Transport ship
Katboth	Essential member(s) of HQ
Kedlairl	Imperial nautical mile
Kenru	School
Kenru Lodair	Officers' School
Kenru Sazoir	Administration School
KfauRound	spoon
Kiigaf	Volcanoes
Kijoth Biborbina Yun	Yunyu 303 Star System
Kilugia	Crown Prince / Princess
Kiseg	Connection chains
Klanraj	Laser light, laser beams
Klanyu	Laser pistols
Knaik Kowikia	Mechanical cleaners
Kreuno	Computer terminal wristband
Ktesh	Grieving Pheasant
Kuro	Control desk
Kutaroev	Decorative sash
Kym	Connection lines

L

Labule	Star Force
Laf	Pearl
Larliin	Gene sponsor; provider of genes
Lartbei	Royal Palace
Lartei	Royal families
Lartei Kryb	Royal House of Kryv
Larth	King
Larth Barker	King Barke
Larth Barker Dusanyu	Dusanyu, King Barke
Larth Kryb	King of Kryv
Lartnei	Queen
Latekrirl	Diamonds
Lef	Landed gentry
Leitfeklash Sufagnaum	Safugnoff Principality Guards
Lesheik Jadbyr	Section Fleet Commander
Lo	Small vessel dock or hatch
Lo Yadobel	Ship's hatch airlock
Lodairl	Pilot; Officer
Loebehynu Sufagnaum	Marquis Safugnoff's territory
Loebeje Sufagnaum	Marquis Safugnoff's family
Loj Febdak	Lady Febdash
Lonid	Base
Lonjhoth Rirrga	Data concatenation
Lonyu	Your / His / Her Excellency
Lonyu Jarluker Dreur	Your / His Excellency the Count's Son
Lonyu Lyum	Your / His Excellency the baron
Lonyu Lyuf Raika	Your / His Excellency the Former Baron
Lowas	Deca-Commander
Lukia	Adjutant
Luode	Telephone-like device
Lyuf	Baron
Lyuf Febdak	Baron Febdash
Lyuf Raika	Former Baron
Lyuf Raika Febdak	Former Baron Febdash
Lyumex	A Baron's mansion
Lyumex Febdak	Baron Febdash's mansion
Lyumjhe Febdak	Baron Febdash's family

Lyumusko	Baron's territory
Lyumusko Febdak	Baron Febdash's territory

M

Menyu	Spaceship(s) (especially Plane Space ships)
Mosk	Pocket

N

Nahen	Land worlds
Nui Abliarsar	The Abriel ears

O

Onhokia	Automatic mechanism
Onyuldiot	
Opdatykirl	Main computer
Opsei	Main engines

P

Parhynu	"Country of Roses"
Partia	Office clerk
Pelia	Coordination vessel, contact vessel
Ponyu	Transport vessel

Q

R

Resii	Patrol ship
Ribeun	Territory
Ribwasia	Paralysis gun
Rodorumzesh	Lava pine
Roibomowas	Vice Hecto-Commander
Roiglaharerl Shutymer	Peace Protection Office Vice Commander
Ronrev	Sand grass
Rue Bitsairl	Imperial subjects
Rue Gryu	Imperial Command Staff
Rue Lef	Imperial citizen
Rue Nigla	Imperial Crest

Rue Spen	Imperial Field Marshal or Imperial Fleet Admiral
Ruecoth	Imperial Year
Ryuazornyu	Military Command HQ
Ryurdauwa	Carbon crystal fiber

S

Saij Daifat Heita	Electromagnetic wave family crest key
Saij Kimena	Code key
Saput	Pressurized helmet
Sarerl	Ship's Captain
Sash	Crew member
Sathoth	Victory
Sathoth Frybareri	Victory for the Empire
Sedia	Pilot
Sei	Engine
Seif Sos	Territorial people's representative
Seif Spauder Rirrag	Intelligence Bureau Chief
Semei Sos	Territorial citizens' government
Serlin	Uniform
Shewas	Kilo-Commander
Shirsh Belysegar	Control Room
Shirsh Sediar	Cockpit
Shirsh Spaurthot Mata	Delivery Room
Shirsh Yokuskurot	Operations Room
Shuteyum Lalbryubu	Lalbryubu Peace Protection Office
Sif	Noble
Skarl	Imperial standard currency
Skemsoraj	Royal throne
Skemsorl	Imperial throne
Skemsorl Roen	Jade Imperial throne
Skobrotaf	Stopped state (in Fath)
Skor	Territory
Sord	Gate between Fath and Dath
Sord Febdak	Febdash Sord
Sord Irik	Iriish Sord
Sord Leza	Closed Sord
Sord Sufagnaum	Safugnoff Sord

Sordlash Elukufar	Milky Way Sord Group
Sorf	Bodysuit, pantsuit
Sorl Bandak	Central Territory
Sorl Geiraza	Unexplored Territory
Sos	Territorial citizens
Soteyua	Computer terminal
Sov Raglaze	Independent squadrons
Sov Vekekar	Fuel tank asteroid
Spaude Rirrag	Intelligence Bureau
Speish	Ring(s)
Speish Dana	Seventh ring
Speish Gana	Eighth ring
Speish Kasna	First ring
Speish Mata	Second ring
Speish Lokeutona	Eleventh ring
Speish Lomata	Twelfth ring
Sperush	Aide
Spunej	Emperor, Empress
Spunej Erumita	Her Majesty the Empress
Spunej Ramaj Erumita	Her Majesty Empress Ramaj
Sune	Court rank or title
Supflasath	Space-time particles

T

Traiga	Noble rank or title

U

Uultaf	Shooting
Uusia	Floating car

V

Voda	Landed nobility
Vodajhe	Voda's family

W

Wabes Bezorlot	Audience Hall
Wabes Lizel	Larkspur Hall
Waloth Ryuazon	Army Commander-in-Chief

Wameria	Gravity control
Waniil	Battlefield meals (MREs)
Wariit	Family characteristic
Was Kasaler	Chief of Staff
Wikreurl	Warship

X

Y

Yadobel	Airlock
Yofuldeal	person

Z

Postscript

I once read somewhere that Robert E. Howard wrote his classic heroic fantasy series by simply transcribing what Conan had said. I'm not inclined to believe in the occult, so I viewed this as an example of the greatness of the unconscious mind. As a student and an aspiring SF writer, I was incredibly envious and wanted to have a similar experience. For one thing, it appealed to me as an easy way to write.

Time passed. Shortly after I'd achieved my short story debut, it happened. On day, as I sat indulging in solitary meditations, sadly gazing at a liquor bottle, a beautiful woman who appeared to be in her mid-twenties danced down before me. Her hair was the color of a deep forest, held in place by a delicate crown, and her eyes were an intimidating jet black.

What luck, I thought. As a healthy young man, I preferred the apparition of a lovely, young female muse to that of a sword-wielding muscleman.

I turned on the Word Processor right away, prepared to accept her story.

"Let's see, can you tell me your name first?" I asked. In response the beautiful woman thrust out her chin and said, "You shall call me Lafiel."

Then, she disappeared. I asked, "Hey, what's your basic story?" but she didn't respond. All I had at hand was her name and the vivid image that remained in my head.

Even so, I wanted to try writing her story. At first she ran wild, completely out of control while I wrote. So I tried sketching out her youth. This was not because I thought a girl would be less complicated than a grown woman, but rather because it would bring order to the story. Of course, it's up to you whether or not to believe that kind of nonsense (laughs). But from time to time, I have to stop and ask myself, *Are these people really just in my head?*

For example, in this second volume, there's a scene in which Jinto and Lafiel are walking. Lafiel's in a bad mood, and no one knows why, not even the author. In my opinion, it's because she'd absorbed some of Jinto's habits. At any rate, all I know is that she's mad about something.

I felt the strangeness of being with the characters. Then, when I looked at it from Lafiel's point of view, I understood exactly why she was upset, and that, if I had her personality, I'd be enraged too. That was a strange experience.

I feel that this volume is simple when compared with the first. However, it's also the volume that contains the author's favorite scene. I won't say which one, even if you ask.

Next up is the last volume: *Return to a Strange World*. In addition to being the climax of the story, there's also a lot of character growth; it's a very crowded volume.

Please enjoy it.
—Hiroyuki Morioka